SETTING SAIL
after SUNDAY MORNING

RON BALL

Tyndale House Publishers, Inc.
WHEATON, ILLINOIS

Visit Tyndale's exciting Web site at www.tyndale.com

ISBN 0-8423-3722-9

Printed in the United States of America

05   04   03   02   01   00
6   5   4   3   2   1

This book is gratefully dedicated to
Dexter Yager Sr. and Charles Stanley,
my mentors in Christ.

Contents

Acknowledgments   vii
Introduction   ix

Chapter 1: Who Is Jesus?   1
Common Misconceptions about Jesus
Incredible Truths about Jesus

Chapter 2: Making A Commitment   19
Steps to a Relationship
Surrendering Control

Chapter 3: Acknowledging the Holy
Spirit   27
The Roles the Spirit Plays

Chapter 4: Developing a Spiritual Root
System   33
Hindrances to Spiritual Growth
Results of Spiritual Growth

Chapter 5: Discovering Your Spiritual
Gifts   43
A Listing of the Gifts
A Last Word about Gifts

Chapter 6: Learning about Prayer   59
Why Should You Pray?
When Should You Pray?
Developing an Attitude of Prayer
The Four Elements of Prayer
Prayer Starters
Six Types of Prayers
How to Know If God Speaks to You

CHAPTER 7: STUDYING YOUR BIBLE 85
Myths about the Bible
Why Make It a Priority?
Practical Steps
Methods of Studying the Bible
Memorizing Bible Verses

CHAPTER 8: SHARING YOUR FAITH 99
What Is Witnessing?
Things to Remember When
Witnessing
A Special Note on Witnessing
to Family Members

CHAPTER 9: CHOOSING THE RIGHT
CHURCH 111
Five Characteristics of a Godly
Church

CHAPTER 10: SO WHAT'S NEXT? 117

CHAPTER 11: HELPS FOR CHRISTIAN
GROWTH 121
Recommended Reading 121
The One Year New Testament
Reading Plan 127
Favorite Bible Passage Index 144
Tyndale Bible Verse Finder 147

ACKNOWLEDGMENTS

I have deeply appreciated the wonderful help of certain key people in the preparation of this book. Thanks to my wife, Amy, and daughter, Allison, for input and support. Thanks to Birdie, Jeff, Steve, and Doyle Yager for invaluable assistance. Thanks especially to Cliff Johnson, Tammy Faxel, and the excellent Tyndale House staff. The expert editorial team at Tyndale played a critical role in the completion of this project; you guys made the difference!

INTRODUCTION

*Do you wish your life had more significance,
more meaning? Does your heart feel empty,
as if something's missing? Do you want to
know if you're good at anything or just
"ordinary"? Do you long to know if there's a
God—and if there is, if He cares about you,
and all the day-to-day things you go
through?*

*Then you're not alone. Hundreds of thou-
sands of others feel the same way. They
wonder on a daily basis why they have been
born into the families they belong to, why
they can't seem to find a job that fits their
personality and gifts (but they don't know
where else to look), and why they have such
a "soul hunger" for more—more confidence,
more and deeper relationships, more knowledge about who they are and how they were
created, and more connection with Someone
higher than them, who understands how the
world and people work.*

*And yet, even in a country that features
the words "In God We Trust" on every coin,
the majority of people don't really under-*

stand who God, or His Son, Jesus Christ, really is. They may think of God as a demanding father who will punish them if they're bad, or as an uncaring or weak father who can't help a world that's spinning out of control. They may think of Jesus as a symbolic Easter figure, along with bunnies, eggs, and baskets.

But those who choose to learn more about God, Jesus, and Christianity will never be sorry. They won't waste their time. I'll guarantee that! And, in fact, the rewards are better than anything you could ever receive on this earth. They're never ending. How?

In this book, I want to set sail with you on a journey to discover and become the best you can be: God's child, full of joy, love, peace, and wisdom. It's a combination that makes for an incredible life, more fulfilling relationships, and soul satisfaction for all eternity!

No matter what stage of "faith" you're in—whether you've been a Christian for years, you've just become a Christian, or you're merely checking out what God and Christianity are all about, this book is intended for you. You'll discover first who Jesus, God's Son, is and examine misconceptions and truths about Him. Then we'll talk about how your response to Jesus can change your life, give you a lifetime relationship with God, help you grow spiritually, discover *your gifts, and learn how to pray (including discerning who's really talking to you—yourself, Satan, or God). Next we'll investigate the myths people swallow about the Bible—and how to find answers to your questions in this incredible Book. In addition, as you learn more about God and Jesus, you'll want to tell others what you're finding out, so I'll give you pointers on how to do just that—and how to find the right church for you. And finally, in order to help you in your life-long journey of faith, I've included some helps for your Christian growth, including recommended reading resources, a one-year reading plan, an index to some great Bible passages that are guaranteed to become your favorites, and an easy "verse finder" to assist you in answering your heartfelt questions.*

Are you ready to set sail—past what you think of as a "typical" Sunday morning at church? Then let's discover together the kind of faith that can transform your life and relationships—for the good!

Ron Ball

CHAPTER ONE

Who Is Jesus?

Who do *you* think Jesus is?

Just ask anybody on the street, and you'll come up with varied answers that range from "He was a good guy who helped people" to "He's a god like Muhammad, right?" to "He's God's Son, who died on the cross for our sins."

No matter where you go, people have an opinion about Jesus. But even those who think they know who Jesus is can be wrong.

For instance, when I was in Pittsburgh a while ago, I was asked to visit a school where drugs were a pressing problem. Our goal was to reach a number of these young men and women who were beginning to damage themselves with drug use and introduce them to Jesus Christ, who could change their lives forever. The auditorium was crowded with kids who were seeking answers, and they responded by the dozen, night after night. They walked to the front of the auditorium to make a public commitment to Christ.

After each night's event, we invited those who had come forward to go with us to the school library. That gave me the opportunity to talk with them about the new life they had chosen and to help them get their relationship with Christ started in the right direction. I wanted to make sure they understood what they had really done at the meeting.

I entered the library full of enthusiasm and began to ask them this question, one-on-one: "What do you think being a Christian means?"

The answers I got were these:

- "Being a Christian is being a good person."
- "Being a Christian is doing what your mom and dad say and being on time for school."
- "Being a Christian is choosing not to break windows, even when you've got the chance."
- "Being nice to people."

After all of these shorter responses, finally one shy girl in the back said, "Well, I think there's something more." I got excited, thinking, *This teen's going to nail it.* She continued, "It's not just being good; it's not just believing in God. It's going to church every Sunday, too." My heart sank. *No,* I thought, *being a Christian is so much more than that.* So I began to explain to them again what it means to know Jesus personally, to accept that He died on the cross as a substitute for their sins, and to have a personal relationship with Him.

Since having a personal relationship with Christ is at the heart of the Christian faith, our first step on the journey is to examine the misconceptions and truths about Him.

Common Misconceptions about Jesus

In order to get to know Him, we have to know first who He *isn't*. Here are nine common misconceptions.

Misconception #1: He's just a curse word. For a lot of people, using Jesus' name in vain—saying "Oh, Jesus Christ!"—is the total extent of their contact with Him. It's amazing—and very sad—that people use the most loving name ever communicated to the human race as a way to express vehemence, violence, and angry emotion.

Today when I hear Jesus' name being used in such a way I wonder: Do they know who He is? Do they know they're talking about the Lord of history? Do they realize they're going to face Him someday and be judged for all eternity? According to Philippians 2:9-11, His name is "above every other name, so that at the name of Jesus every knee will bow, in heaven and on earth and under the earth, and every tongue will confess that Jesus Christ is Lord, to the glory of God the Father."

A good rule to remember is this: When you say someone's name—either in kindness or as a curse word—you get his or her attention.

Misconception #2: He's an outdated fairy tale.

Some believe Jesus is a myth, a legendary figure who may have lived but probably didn't. He's like Paul Bunyan and Sleeping Beauty—storybook characters who are OK for children but not for grown-ups who have details to manage, relationships to juggle, and jobs to do and who want to succeed in life.

What about you? Do you see Him as an unreal character who's not in touch with reality, history, or the world today or who belongs only in the pages of a dusty, out-of-use Bible?

Misconception #3: He's just a crutch for children and old people.

Some people believe Jesus is a way of getting through life for those who are too weak to make it otherwise. They can lean on religion until they're tough, mature, and successful enough to make it on their own. Then they won't need Jesus. He's for Sunday school children and those who are widowed or sick or poor.

This is one of the nastiest misconceptions, sent from Satan himself, to keep you from seeking a relationship with Jesus. The truth is that everyone needs Him, including you and me.

Misconception #4: He's a threat, and He makes you feel guilty.

Those who see Jesus as a threatening, disturbing symbol of religious guilt live their whole lives as if they are walking on an emotional and spiritual tightrope over the fires of hell. If their balance on the tightrope of guilt becomes too precarious, they'll be plunged into the flames below. And to make it worse, they worry that if they're not good enough morally or kind enough to others, He'll put pressure on the rope to cause them to fall. And they're helpless—there's nothing they can do to save themselves.

The truth is that you *can't* do anything to save yourself: Christ has already done it! All you need to do is accept it. This book will show you how.

Misconception #5: He's a sour reminder of unlikable people and unpleasant pressure.

Today's media does a lot to portray Christians as judgmental, backward, narrow, and unloving. For instance, on one TV show that dealt with homosexuality, transvestism, and various other sexual perversions, there was only one man—who said he was a Christian—who took a stand against such evil. But the problem was, he was the meanest person in the whole group.

What did that communicate except the sad misconception that all people who wear the name of Jesus will jump at the opportunity to point accusing fingers? But that's not how the Bible says Christians should act. Although it's true of some Christians (and I wish it were not), it's not a right picture of what God says Christians ought to be.

Have you ever known someone who said he was a Christian and then treated you badly? The next time you heard that someone was a Christian, what happened in your mind? Most likely, you thought instantly of that first rude or mean person. And then you told yourself, *I don't think I want to get to know this second person because she's probably like the first Christian I met.*

Because of these bad examples, Jesus often becomes a symbol of sourness, of unlikable people, and of unpleasant pressure. But the real Jesus is far different from that.

Misconception #6: He's nothing but a superstitious good-luck charm.

Some people view "religious" symbols, including Jesus, as a way to ward off evil and increase their good fortune—almost like a rabbit's foot.

Once when I was on a trip, I visited one such lady. Although her home was filled with religious symbols and she used "Christian" lingo, I soon realized that these symbols were used to "ward off" evil. She actually lived in great fear and dread of what might happen to her.

And she's not the only one. Many people own Bibles, but they don't really read or study them. Instead, they assume having one will shield them and/or their families from misfortune, illness, bad debt, bankruptcy, and even the devil's influence.

But if Jesus is a merely good-luck charm to you, then you'll never know the vitality of His power or His full plan of who you can be in Him.

Misconception #7: He's just an object of religious respect.

Those who see Jesus as only an object of religious veneration can walk into church or Mass, quietly and full of humility, sing songs, and repeat words, but they never touch God. As a result, it's easier to leave Him in the sanctuary or cathedral and go about their business during the week, then pick Him up again the next Saturday or Sunday. As for the rest of the week, anything can go—including gossiping, cheating on their taxes or in business, hanging out in bad company, having an affair, verbally abusing their children, etc. They live lives that are not spiritually right because Jesus is not real to them—He's just a distant symbol.

Is Jesus a part of your daily life, or only on Saturday or Sunday?

Misconception #8: He's a last resort in desperate times.

There are those who don't look to Jesus until a problem is too big to handle on their own—for instance, terminal cancer, bankruptcy, divorce, or a child's addiction to drugs. When nothing else works, Jesus becomes that last hope. In essence, He's an insurance policy when they have to pull out all the stops.

But those who don't care about God and His principles and values are being hypocritical when they ask Him to save them at the last moment. They don't want to give up control until they have to—until it's too late to save themselves. God is not real enough to them, and so they miss the power and the explosive reality of peace and joy that come when He's the first, rather than last, resort in their life.

However, what's important to remember is that, even if you call on Him as a last resort and ask Him to save you and come into your life, He'll respond. But then you'll have to endure the pain of all the wasted years you lived without Him. So why not try Him first, rather than last?

Misconception #9: He's a mystery.

For most people in America and all over the world, Jesus is someone they don't understand. He's a mystery. Where did He come from? Who created Him? How can He, who has been dead for almost two thousand years, still have such an impact on His followers today?

What about you? Is He a mystery to you? Are you curious enough to delve in, trying to discover more about Him, the way He lived, came back from the dead, ascended to heaven, and now greatly affects our lives today?

If so, you're on your way, and this book will help you!

INCREDIBLE TRUTHS ABOUT JESUS

Now that we've listed the misconceptions about Jesus, we turn to the truths about this Person. Who is He? Certainly not just a good man or merely a great religious leader or teacher. He's not simply the founder of Christianity. He's more than all that.

Using verses from the Bible, God's Word about Himself and His acts, let's examine nine key truths about who Jesus is.

Truth #1: He's God in human form.
The awesome truth is that Jesus Christ is God Himself! In the Gospel of John in the New Testament, He said, "The Father [God] and I are one" (John 10:30). Jesus is God in human form—God in human flesh—as these verses show.

9

Christ is the head of the church, which is his body. He is the first of all who will rise from the dead, so he is first in everything. For God in all his fullness was pleased to live in Christ, and by him God reconciled everything to himself. He made peace with everything in heaven and on earth by means of his blood on the cross.

COLOSSIANS 1:18-20

Though he was God, he did not demand and cling to his rights as God. He made himself nothing; he took the humble position of a slave and appeared in human form. And in human form he obediently humbled himself even further by dying a criminal's death on a cross.

PHILIPPIANS 2:6-8

Truth #2: He's a living, breathing person. Jesus is real, and He's alive right now in heaven, watching all you do.

First John 1:1 states: "The one who existed from the beginning is the one we have heard and seen. We saw him with our own eyes and touched him with our own hands. He is Jesus Christ, the Word of life." In this verse, the apostle John is saying, in everyday language, "Hey! This Jesus, who has always lived, who will live forever—He invaded history and I touched Him! I talked to Him, I lived with Him, I knew Him."

Jesus experienced sorrow, laughter, pain,

betrayal, hunger, stress, and tiredness, just as you do. Because of that, He's able to understand your struggles. Hebrews 4:13-16 says:

Nothing in all creation can hide from him. Everything is naked and exposed before his eyes. This is the God to whom we must explain all that we have done.

That is why we have a great High Priest who has gone to heaven, Jesus the Son of God. Let us cling to him and never stop trusting him. This High Priest of ours understands our weaknesses, for he faced all of the same temptations we do, yet he did not sin. So let us come boldly to the throne of our gracious God. There we will receive his mercy, and we will find grace to help us when we need it.

Truth #3: He's the only one who can forgive you of your sins and remove your guilt. People all over America live with guilt every day, and it translates into increasing pressure, tension, bouts of anger or anxiety, and even depression. Jesus Christ is the only one who can forgive you. Because Jesus paid the penalty for your sins when He died on the cross, God can pronounce you completely forgiven.

For God so loved the world that he gave his only Son, so that everyone who believes in him will not perish but have eternal life. God did not send his Son into the world to condemn it, but to save it.

JOHN 3:16-17

When you turn from your sins and accept that Jesus took your punishment by dying on the cross, God will forgive you. But that doesn't mean you go out and say, "Oh, hooray! I'm now forgiven!" and live any way you please. If that's true—if you continue on the same path you were going previously—then you've never really come to know and love Jesus. When you're a follower of Jesus Christ, you want to show your love to Him through the way you act, talk, and think. He will give you the power to break the hold of selfishness and sin in your life.

If we say we have no sin, we are only fooling ourselves and refusing to accept the truth. But if we confess our sins to him, he is faithful and just to forgive us and to cleanse us from every wrong.

1 JOHN 1:8-9

Truth #4: He's the only one who totally understands you, loves you anyway, and wants to help you.

John 2:25 says it bluntly, "No one needed to tell him [Jesus] about human nature." That means Jesus knows you totally—your good points, your bad points. He knows how you were knit together in your mother's womb,

12

what struggles you've had, and what will happen in your future. And since He lived on earth, he knows the temptations you face and can help you to resist them and their sad consequences. So why not accept the twenty-four-hour-a-day companionship of the only Person who understands you completely, wants to help you, and loves you more intensely than anyone else ever could?

> *We all know that Jesus came to help the descendants of Abraham, not to help the angels. Therefore, it was necessary for Jesus to be in every respect like us, his brothers and sisters, so that he could be our merciful and faithful High Priest before God. He then could offer a sacrifice that would take away the sins of the people. Since he himself has gone through suffering and temptation, he is able to help us when we are being tempted.*
>
> HEBREWS 2:16-18

Truth #5: He's the only one who can make any relationship work God's way.
Without Christ, you can have a tolerably good relationship with a sister, coworker, spouse, etc. But you cannot know all that God intended for each of you without Jesus as the center of your life. Why? He's the only one who can break the power of selfishness and release the powerful principles that solidify relationships and also heal hurting ones.

Wisdom about relationships is peppered throughout the Bible. Here are just a few of the selections:

> *You have heard that the law of Moses says, "Love your neighbor" and hate your enemy. But I say, love your enemies! Pray for those who persecute you!*
>
> MATTHEW 5:43-44

> *Even if he wrongs you seven times a day and each time turns again and asks forgiveness, forgive him.*
>
> LUKE 17:4

> *Love is patient and kind. Love is not jealous or boastful or proud or rude. Love does not demand its own way. Love is not irritable, and it keeps no record of when it has been wronged. It is never glad about injustice but rejoices whenever the truth wins out. Love never gives up, never loses faith, is always hopeful, and endures through every circumstance.*
>
> 1 CORINTHIANS 13:4-7

> *Make me truly happy by agreeing wholeheartedly with each other, loving one another, and working together with one heart and purpose.*
>
> *Don't be selfish; don't live to make a good impression on others. Be humble, thinking of others as better than yourself. Don't think only about your own affairs,*

*but be interested in others, too, and what
they are doing.*

*Your attitude should be the same that
Christ Jesus had.* PHILIPPIANS 2:2-5

Truth #6: He's the source of a successful life.
In John 10:10, Jesus said, "My purpose is to
give life in all its fullness." That means that,
as a Christian, your life will overflow with
goodness and soul-healthy living. When you
follow God's laws and live with the love of
Jesus in your heart, He will change your relationships, your activities, and your business.
God has a purpose and a plan for you.

*You must be even more careful to put into
action God's saving work in your lives,
obeying God with deep reverence and
fear. For God is working in you, giving
you the desire to obey him and the power
to do what pleases him.*

PHILIPPIANS 2:12-13

*I keep working toward that day when I
will finally be all that Christ Jesus saved
me for and wants me to be.*

PHILIPPIANS 3:12

Truth #7: He's supreme over all creation.
Not only does Jesus know *you* inside and
out, He knows *everything* inside and out.
Why? Because God the Father gave Him
control over all creation. Only He can count
the number of atoms in the universe; only He

understands everything there is to know about the earth. And that means He's supreme over everything that exists, including you!

> *Christ is the visible image of the invisible God. He existed before God made anything at all and is supreme over all creation. Christ is the one through whom God created everything in heaven and earth. He made the things we can see and the things we can't see—kings, kingdoms, rulers, and authorities. Everything has been created through him and for him. He existed before everything else began, and he holds all creation together.*
>
> COLOSSIANS 1:15-17

Truth #8: He's the only one in the universe who has power over life and death.
No matter what age or stage of life we're in today, we will all die someday. And money, success, and youth are meaningless without God as a focus for your life.

Scripture makes it clear that Jesus Christ is the only door to heaven. Ephesians 1:19-20 states, "I pray that you will begin to understand the incredible greatness of his power for us who believe him. This is the same mighty power that raised Christ from the dead and seated him in the place of honor at God's right hand in the heavenly realms." If you are a follower of Jesus, you have tremendous power in your life: Death will not stop you because you know the One who is the bridge beyond death.

> *So you see, just as death came into the world through a man, Adam, now the resurrection from the dead has begun through another man, Christ. Everyone dies because all of us are related to Adam, the first man. But all who are related to Christ, the other man, will be given new life.*
>
> 1 CORINTHIANS 15:21-22

> *Our perishable earthly bodies must be transformed into heavenly bodies that will never die.*
> *When this happens—when our perishable earthly bodies have been transformed into heavenly bodies that will never die— then at last the Scriptures will come true:*
> *"Death is swallowed up in victory. O death, where is your victory? O death, where is your sting?"*
>
> 1 CORINTHIANS 15:53-55

Truth #9: He has the power to transform people.

Through the power of Christ, an ordinary person can become extraordinary. People who are shy and unassuming, who find it difficult to talk to others about anything, can be made bold by the cause of Christ. Acts 4:13

gives an account of how a Christ-filled life transforms a person.

> *The members of the council were amazed when they saw the boldness of Peter and John, for they could see that they were ordinary men who had had no special training. They also recognized them as men who had been with Jesus.*

The wonderful, absolute truth is that Jesus can transform your life. He is real. He is God, the Source of love, peace, joy, forgiveness, and the Key to an incredible, fulfilling life. He is the only way to know God, the way to forgiveness, the way to healthy relationships, the way to eternal life, the way to transforming your life. Why? Because Jesus is life itself! As John 14:6-7 says: "I am the way, the truth, and the life. No one can come to the Father except through me. If you had known who I am, then you would have known who my Father is. From now on you know him and have seen him!" Jesus, the Son of God, is God Himself. As you get to know Him, you get to know the Father.

CHAPTER TWO

Making a Commitment

Are you interested in a changed life—a life that will give you fulfillment, meaning, and satisfaction galore? Although the Christian life is not without its problems—for instance, you may still suffer the consequences of your wrongdoing—deciding to accept Jesus Christ into your life means that you'll never be alone again. The Jesus we read about in chapter 1, who knows you, loves you, and understands you better than anyone else, will be walking with you.

You may—or may not—know Christ personally yet. If, after the previous chapter, you're convinced that Jesus is the Son of God and that He died for your sins, you're ready to decide whether or not you want to take the next step: making a lifelong commitment to walking with Him.

STEPS TO A RELATIONSHIP

How do you enter into a relationship with Jesus? Just follow these four steps to a changed life.

1. Believe that Jesus is who He says He is— God.

You may be Jewish, Muslim, Buddhist, Protestant, or Catholic, but none of those labels change the absolute truth that Jesus Christ is the only way to God. In Galatians 3:22, the apostle Paul writes, "But the Scriptures have declared that we are all prisoners of sin, so the only way to receive God's promise is to believe in Jesus Christ."

If you'd like to study this part of having a relationship with Jesus Christ further, see "Recommended Reading" on page 121.

2. Admit your sin.

You may think, *I'm not a bad person—I don't steal or murder or cheat or break any of the other Ten Commandments.* But the truth is that everyone is a sinner. No one is good enough when stacked up next to the perfect, all-knowing, almighty God of the universe. And no one can save himself. We need the ultimate sacrifice—God's Son, who died on the cross as a substitute for us. The Bible says:

> *If we say we have no sin, we are only fooling ourselves and refusing to accept the truth. But if we confess our sins to him, he is faithful and just to forgive us and to cleanse us from every wrong. If we claim we have not sinned, we are calling*

God a liar and showing that his word has no place in our hearts.   I JOHN 1:8-10

3. Repent from your sin.

When you repent, you don't just say you'll never do that action again. It means you actually turn away from your sin and have a change of attitude. With Christ walking alongside you, you won't want to commit that sin again (and if you do, your heart will be sorely grieved and your soul will be pricked with a guilty conscience from the Holy Spirit, whom Christ sends to live within you when you become a Christian).

If you believe that your actions—good deeds, baptism, going to church or Mass, believing in God, or giving money—will get you into heaven, you're sadly mistaken. Although those things are all good, they are useless if you have not repented and asked Jesus to forgive you for the sin in your life. When you repent of your sin, Jesus says that you

turn from darkness to light, and from the power of Satan to God. Then [you] will receive forgiveness for [your] sins and be given a place among God's people, who are set apart by faith in me.   ACTS 26:18

4. Receive Jesus as the Guard, Guide, and Savior of your life.

This is an act of your will and personal trust and faith in Him. Accept His death and resurrection for you. Believe that He died, not just for the whole human race, but for you, and that He rose from the dead for you. That's how much He loves you and wants to be the center of your life!

A relationship with Jesus Christ is a free gift—the only thing you have to do is accept it. Jesus gives you a clear invitation:

> *Look! Here I stand at the door and knock. If you hear me calling and open the door, I will come in, and we will share a meal as friends.*   REVELATION 3:20

When Jesus says He wants to "share a meal as friends," he's talking about an intimate, close friendship, one of the many benefits of a life with Christ. Only Jesus can give you true joy, peace, love, and eternal life—and it's a free gift. Now that's the best investment you could ever make!

If you agree with the four points above, you're ready to make a decision. Will you choose to follow Christ?

If so, pray, asking Him to come into your life. It doesn't have to be a fancy prayer—after all, praying is just talking with God. Even this simple prayer will do:

> Jesus, I believe You are the Son of God, who died for my sins. And I know I'm a sinner. Please forgive me of my sins. Take charge of my life, for I want to serve You. Amen.

If you say this prayer and mean it, you've just begun a new life. Jesus said that you are spiritually "born again" when you make the decision to follow Him as Lord and Savior (see John 3:1-10). This means that Jesus becomes the number-one priority in your life, and you make changes and decisions in your life according to the direction He has given you in the Bible. In essence, you "surrender control" to Him—in every area of your life.

Surrendering Control

Several years ago I was speaking at a youth camp in Illinois to over four hundred teen-agers. It was a thrilling time because these teens seemed excited to discover more about Jesus. So after I'd talked about who He was, and how He could change their lives, I invited them to respond publicly. Dozens of young men and women came from all over the auditorium to pray, to make a commitment to follow Jesus Christ.

One young sixteen-year-old in particular left a vivid impression in my mind. Attractive and well liked, she was so prominent in every activity in the camp that I'd already gotten to know her. But since she had seemed eager to be involved in every aspect of camp and had seemed "spiritually mature," I wondered why she had come in tears to the front to surrender control of her life to Christ.

As I knelt down in front of her and asked her what I could pray with her about, she cried even harder. Finally she took a deep breath, looked up at me with teary eyes, and said, "Last year I came to this same camp and prayed at this same spot to become a Christian."

"Why are you back?" I asked gently.

"Well," she said, "when I went home, I knew that I needed to grow spiritually, but I didn't feel like it. Once I wasn't in the camp setting, I didn't feel like reading my Bible, so I didn't. I didn't feel like praying, so I didn't. I didn't feel like responding obediently to my mother or father as a Christian should, so I didn't. I struggled with my commitment for about four days and finally decided that being a Christian wasn't worth it. It was too much work, and I didn't want to be disciplined. I didn't want to form the right habits, so I just didn't do it. So here I am, having had a year of spiritual failure. Why? What's wrong with me?"

I told her what I'm going to tell you regarding spiritual growth. First, she needed to make a commitment that was really a commitment, not merely a "caught up in the moment" statement that would disappear as soon as the camp was over. Second, she needed to acknowledge the new Person in her life—the Holy Spirit—and let Him guide her (see chapter 3). Third, she needed to develop a spiritual root system (chapter 4).

Because we're human, it's easy to forget that, after your initial decision to accept Christ, your work isn't done. You need to actively choose to walk with Christ. And that's what the rest of this book is all about.

CHAPTER THREE

Acknowledging the Holy Spirit

The heart of the gospel is knowing Jesus personally and powerfully. And as soon as you surrender control of your life to Him, God sends His Holy Spirit to help you—to guide your thoughts, actions, and decisions.

What is the Holy Spirit? The Holy Spirit is not a thing, an "it," or a ghost. The Bible refers to Him as a person. In chapters 14 through 17 of the book of John, in the New Testament, Jesus refers to him as the "Counselor" or "Comforter": "If you love me, obey my commandments. And I will ask the Father, and he will give you another Counselor, who will never leave you. He is the Holy Spirit, who leads into all truth. . . . He lives with you now and later will be in you" (John 14:15-17).

The Bible also teaches that the Holy Spirit is part of the "Trinity"—God, Jesus, and the Holy Spirit (see Matthew 28:19). What does that mean? Although God is one unity, He exists in three distinct persons:

27

God the Father, Jesus the Son, and the Holy Spirit. If this sounds confusing to you, you're not alone. How this can be possible is a vast mystery that all people—including theologians—have been trying to figure out for centuries. Although we may not understand it on earth, someday it will be explained to us in heaven. The simplest way to explain it is this: God the Father is Creator, Sustainer, and Commander in Chief. God the Son is Savior, Lord, and Intercessor. God the Holy Spirit is Guide, Helper, and Counselor.

THE ROLES THE SPIRIT PLAYS

In essence, the Holy Spirit plays these roles in a Christian's life:

He helps you in your day-to-day walk with God.

The Holy Spirit serves as your guide and conscience. Romans 8:26 puts it this way: "And the Holy Spirit helps us in our distress. For we don't even know what we should pray for, nor how we should pray. But the Holy Spirit prays for us with groanings that cannot be expressed in words." In other words, the Spirit knows even those inner yearnings—even when you can't express them. The Holy Spirit searches your heart and "pleads for us believers in harmony with God's own will" (Romans 8:27).

He gives you confidence that you are God's child and will share His inheritance.

Romans 8:15-17 states it bluntly:

> So you should not be like cowering, fearful slaves. You should behave instead like God's very own children, adopted into his family—calling him "Father, dear Father." For his Holy Spirit speaks to us deep in our hearts and tells us that we are God's children. And since we are his children, we will share his treasures—for everything God gives to his Son, Christ, is ours, too.

He is active in your conversion.

No one can become a Christian without the power of the Holy Spirit's work in his life because the Spirit is who does the changing. Romans 8:9 says:

> But you are not controlled by your sinful nature. You are controlled by the Spirit if you have the Spirit of God living in you. (And remember that those who do not have the Spirit of Christ living in them are not Christians at all.)

In other words, when you ask Jesus Christ to come into your life, a supernatural transaction occurs: The Holy Spirit enters and "fills you"—He begins to make you a new person. At that point you'll still be a spiritual infant, and sometimes this will be obvious. But little by little, God's active agent—the

Spirit—moves and works in your life. Think of Him as God in action. The Holy Spirit's primary work is in your heart—to make you more like Jesus. Although you're still you, you become more Christlike every day—you are more patient, kind, loving, gentle, etc. (in the Bible these are called the "fruit of the Spirit"), and that's crucial to your spiritual development.

Without being "filled" by the Holy Spirit's involvement in your life and decisions, your conversion would not be complete. As Ephesians 4:21-24 says:

> *Since you have heard all about him and have learned the truth that is in Jesus, throw off your old evil nature and your former way of life, which is rotten through and through, full of lust and deception. Instead, there must be a spiritual renewal of your thoughts and attitudes. You must display a new nature because you are a new person, created in God's likeness— righteous, holy, and true.*

Having the Holy Spirit's influence in your life means that you no longer choose to sin, for that grieves God.

> *"Don't sin by letting anger gain control over you." Don't let the sun go down while you are still angry, for anger gives a mighty foothold to the Devil.*

*If you are a thief, stop stealing. Begin
using your hands for honest work, and
then give generously to others in need.
Don't use foul or abusive language. Let
everything you say be good and helpful,
so that your words will be an encouragement to those who hear them.*

*And do not bring sorrow to God's
Holy Spirit by the way you live. Remember, he is the one who has identified you
as his own, guaranteeing that you will be
saved on the day of redemption.*

*Get rid of all bitterness, rage, anger,
harsh words, and slander, as well as all
types of malicious behavior. Instead, be
kind to each other, tenderhearted, forgiv-
ing one another, just as God through
Christ has forgiven you.*   EPHESIANS 4:26-32

*Let there be no sexual immorality, impu-
rity, or greed among you. Such sins have
no place among God's people. Obscene
stories, foolish talk, and coarse jokes—
these are not for you. Instead, let there be
thankfulness to God.*   EPHESIANS 5:3-4

Being *filled* (the word actually means "to
be flooded") with the Spirit means that you
act in a manner that would please God.
Although the Spirit comes into your life automatically when you become a Christian, ask
Him to continue to shape you, so that the

words of Ephesians 5:15-20 will ring true in your life:

> *So be careful how you live, not as fools but as those who are wise. Make the most of every opportunity for doing good in these evil days. Don't act thoughtlessly, but try to understand what the Lord wants you to do. Don't be drunk with wine, because that will ruin your life. Instead, let the Holy Spirit fill and control you. Then you will sing psalms and hymns and spiritual songs among yourselves, making music to the Lord in your hearts. And you will always give thanks for everything to God the Father in the name of our Lord Jesus Christ.*

CHAPTER FOUR

Developing a Spiritual
Root System

Some of you have come to know Jesus in the last year. Others of you have known Him a long time but haven't felt the power and closeness to God that you have hoped and prayed for. You've wanted great spiritual power released in your life, but you haven't known how to get it.

Others of you have met Christ recently, and all of this talk about spiritual growth and God and heaven and the Bible sounds like a foreign language to you.

No matter what your age or stage in the Christian life, it's crucial that you learn how to develop spiritual roots. Why? Here's what the apostle Paul said in Colossians 2:6-7:

> *And now, just as you accepted Christ Jesus as your Lord, you must continue to live in obedience to him. Let your roots grow down into him and draw up nourishment from him, so you will grow in faith, strong and vigorous in the truth you were taught. Let your lives overflow with thanksgiving for all he has done.*

Without a deep, pervading root system that brings in nutrients and water from the earth, a tree will wither and die. The same is true for your spiritual growth: Without strong roots, your faith can begin to wither and die in "dry," difficult times.

HINDRANCES TO SPIRITUAL GROWTH

Not all people who become Christians flourish. Here are four reasons why their roots stop growing—and what can be done about it.

Hindrance #1: Laziness

When you're forming habits and disciplines, growth doesn't come automatically. It's something you have to work for. Second Peter 3:18 says, "Grow in the special favor and knowledge of our Lord and Savior Jesus Christ." The emphasis in that verse is on the word *grow*. The word used in Greek—the original language of Peter's letter—is an active word that means you throw your heart into growing. You don't just lie on your back, smile, and say, "Okay, God, I'm ready. Now grow me." Instead you cooperate with God. You say no to laziness and yes to actively working on your spiritual life. That means you read the Bible even when you don't feel like it, and you get out of bed to go to church even when you're tired.

God expects you to make a commitment to grow, so don't be short-circuited by laziness. Deeply desire God's movement in your life—and then throw your heart, mind, body, and spirit into it!

Hindrance #2: Sin

If there is sin in your life—an area of disobedience to God—your growth will stop.
Maybe you have a habit, an attitude, or a relationship that God has told you isn't right. You know you shouldn't be doing it, but you don't let go of it.

In John 15:9-11, Jesus says:

> *I have loved you even as the Father has loved me. Remain in my love. When you obey me, you remain in my love, just as I obey my Father and remain in his love. I have told you this so that you will be filled with my joy. Yes, your joy will overflow!*

When you refuse to obey God—to remain in his love—you are choosing to halt your growth. Sin dulls your appetite for God. And disobedience in any part of your life will slow your spiritual progress. You cannot afford to let that happen.

Hindrance #3: A lack of awareness

The third reason you can fail to develop a spiritual root system is because you just don't realize the need to do it. You think that when you make a commitment, all of your problems will vanish. You see the Christian life as an "instant fix."

But think of it this way: In all areas of life—your friendships, marriage or dating relationship, work—you have to work if you want success. The same principle applies to your spiritual life: To have spiritual success, you have to actively build a relationship with God. To flourish as a Christian, you must consciously choose to grow.

Hindrance #4: Wrong priorities

If something is a top priority to you, you'll put it first, right? So if you want spiritual growth, but it's not important enough to you to make it a priority, what happens? You'll put everything else—family, friends, work, social life, etc.—ahead of your relationship with God.

In Luke 9:23-25, Jesus describes the kind of priority He should have in your life:

> *If any of you wants to be my follower, you must put aside your selfish ambition, shoulder your cross daily, and follow me. If you try to keep your life for yourself, you will lose it. But if you give up your life for me, you will find true life. And how do you benefit if you gain the whole world but lose or forfeit your own soul in the process?*

When God is in His right place in your life—your first priority—everything else will flow naturally. That doesn't mean you shouldn't work hard at your job or something else. But it does mean that God, through Jesus Christ, comes first in your life.

RESULTS OF SPIRITUAL GROWTH

What happens when you make developing a spiritual root system a priority? Check out these five wonderful results:

Result #1: You'll know God more intimately. If you've accepted Jesus' death on the cross for you, have come to a personal relationship with Him, and are determined to make Him number one in your life, it only makes sense that you'll want to get to know Him better. And nothing in the world can be a substitute for knowing God!

Look at 2 Peter 3:18 again: "Grow in the special favor and knowledge of our Lord and Savior Jesus Christ." The Greek word used here for *knowledge* refers to an intimate, personal relationship. It implies a closeness—that you know a lot about a person.

Every morning when I wake up, the most precious, vital moments of my day are those I spend alone with God. Why? Because I experience His presence, we communicate, and I learn to know Him better.

The better you know God, the more whole and fulfilled you'll become as a person.

Result #2: You'll gain spiritual strength to face life's problems.

Throughout life things will go wrong: You'll experience problems, the death of loved ones, the loss of a job, difficult transitions. But when you have a spiritual root system, the Holy Spirit's power will flow into your life, and you will have His wisdom and peace to deal with these problems. Then, instead of being helplessly battered by the storms of life, you will have direction and peace. You will have a steady resource—spiritual power and godly solutions to life's problems—to help you battle depression, anxiety, dread, and fear.

When you face trouble, turn to God's Word. Psalm 119, for instance, is the heart cry of a man whose life was dedicated to God. Although he still faced problems, he didn't have to give in because he had spiritual power by staying close to God.

> *Happy are people of integrity, who follow the law of the Lord. Happy are those who obey his decrees and search for him with all their hearts. They do not compromise with evil, and they walk only in his paths.* PSALM 119:1-3

Result #3: You'll learn about biblical success and prosperity.

One of the reasons I love the book of Proverbs in the Old Testament so much is because it is a blueprint of how life actually works—how we can make our life a success in God's eyes. How wonderful that God, the Creator of all life, has outlined in the Bible the way His world should work! When you follow His principles, He will bless you with success, and you will prosper in your personal life because of your relationship with Him. That doesn't mean your life will be perfect, because there's still sin in the world. But you'll have an inner contentment that will make you a success by God's definition—no matter what you face in your life.

As Proverbs 21:21 says: "Whoever pursues godliness and unfailing love will find life, godliness, and honor."

Result #4: You'll be protected from evil. Let's not be fooled by cute caricatures of a little red man with red pajamas. Satan exists, and he's a real devil. In fact, the Greek word for Satan is *satanas*, which means "the adversary" or "the enemy." Satan has tremendous intelligence and power, and he uses it to fight God. That means that if you're a Christian, he's viciously opposed to your spiritual growth and development. He'll throw anything and everything in your way to trip you up and keep you far from God.

But that doesn't mean he's all-powerful. And with the Spirit's help, Satan doesn't have to have the last word. As 1 Corinthians 10:13 says:

> *But remember that the temptations that come into your life are no different from what others experience. And God is faithful. He will keep the temptation from becoming so strong that you can't stand up against it. When you are tempted, he will show you a way out so that you will not give in to it.*

As you develop a root system, you'll learn how to better protect yourself from Satan and his lies. You'll learn how to look at relationships, entertainment, books, situations, and places and discern if—and how—they could hurt your relationship with God. As you learn to decipher what's right and wrong through studying the Bible and asking the Holy Spirit to help you in your choices, you'll protect yourself and your loved ones from temptation and Satan's influence.

Result #5: You'll be preparing for heaven. Surprise! When you develop a spiritual root system, you're actually making preparations for your future home in heaven. Although God cares about the here and now, it's important to remember that our lives on earth are just a brief moment compared to eternity. In heaven you'll spend forever with God!

That's why Matthew 6:19-21 says:

Don't store up treasures here on earth, where they can be eaten by moths and get rusty, and where thieves break in and steal. Store your treasures in heaven, where they will never become moth-eaten or rusty and where they will be safe from thieves. Wherever your treasure is, there your heart and thoughts will also be.

How do you store up treasures in heaven? By communicating with God, obeying His Word, and spreading the love of Christ to others through your words and actions. Investing in these types of treasures will bring you much more joy than you could ever imagine!

Now that you know what hinders spiritual growth and its tremendous results, how do you go about developing a spiritual root system?

That's what the rest of this book will show you. You'll learn about spiritual gifts (and begin to discover yours), prayer, Bible study, sharing your faith, and even how to choose the right church for you.

CHAPTER FIVE

Discovering Your
Spiritual Gifts

Do you wish you had a particular gift that
makes you special? Well, you do! As soon as
you accept Jesus into your heart, the Holy
Spirit comes to live there, and God grants you
one or more spiritual gifts. Depending on
how you count them in the Bible, there are
many gifts of the Spirit, including the word of
knowledge, word of wisdom, discernment of
spirits, gifts of healings, speaking in tongues,
interpretation of tongues, administration,
service, teaching, etc.

Why are the gifts of the Spirit important
in a believer's life? Martin Luther, the great
reformer and composer of hymns (including
"A Mighty Fortress Is Our God"), put it this
way: "The Spirit and the gifts are ours
through Him who with us sideth." When you
have Jesus Christ in your heart, in your life as
your Savior, you have the power of the Holy
Spirit within you. Otherwise, if you don't
know Him, the gifts of the Spirit will be a
giant puzzle to you.

43

What are the gifts of the Spirit? They're not just talents or abilities; they're beyond that. For instance, you may have incredible talent for playing the piano, even stirring people's emotions. But it doesn't necessarily mean the Holy Spirit has worked through that music. However, if the Holy Spirit is working through what you do, then what you play will have the added dimension of spiritual power that cannot be explained in merely emotional, human terms. That's why the word *gifts* is related to the Greek word used for God's grace, *karis*—something God freely gives for a specific purpose.

The apostle Paul says this about spiritual gifts in 1 Corinthians 12:4-7:

> *There are different kinds of spiritual gifts, but it is the same Holy Spirit who is the source of them all. There are different kinds of service in the church, but it is the same Lord we are serving. There are different ways God works in our lives, but it is the same God who does the work through all of us. A spiritual gift is given to each of us as a means of helping the entire church.*

So the Bible is clear that gifts of the Spirit are given for the common good, not for the inflation of your ego. In other words, God doesn't bless you with a gift so you can think you're spiritually superior. Unfortunately, this is a mistake many Christians make—and their arrogant behavior can become offensive to others.

The Bible also makes it clear that, while we are each given a gift, none of us will possess all of the gifts of the Spirit. First Corinthians 12:6 says, "There are different ways God works in our lives, but it is the same God who does the work through all of us." The obvious implication of that introduction is that these gifts operate at different levels for different reasons at different times for different people. In other words, not everyone has every gift of the Spirit.

Verses 29-30 continue this argument:

Is everyone an apostle? Of course not. Is everyone a prophet? No. Are all teachers? Does everyone have the power to do miracles? Does everyone have the gift of healing? Of course not. Does God give all of us the ability to speak in unknown languages? Can everyone interpret unknown languages? No!

Then the passage goes on to say, "you should desire the most helpful gifts" and leads directly into the great "love chapter" of 1 Corinthians.

So we should each use the gift God has given us to glorify Him and not seek to possess all the gifts.

A LISTING OF THE GIFTS

What are the key passages on the gifts of the Spirit? Although there are other references to gifts, the three major passages are: 1 Corinthians 12–14; Romans 12; and Ephesians 4.

As we look at each of the eighteen gifts mentioned in these passages, see if you can recognize the gift(s) you have.

#1: The Word of Wisdom

Coming from the Greek words *logos sophias*, the word of wisdom means that God gives you a remarkable insight. For example, you're able to "see" into the root cause of a particular situation.

If you want God to reveal to you why you do certain things, then you need this word of wisdom from Him. So pray and ask Him to shed light on a specific situation. But realize that wisdom doesn't always come in a flash. The gift of the word of wisdom operates for specific reasons at specific times for the common good. So you can't say, "Well, I don't have to read my Bible or pray; I'll just wait for God to drop words of wisdom on me when I need them."

The Bible makes it clear—especially through the book of Proverbs—that God also reveals wisdom slowly. That's why we need to be diligent about reading such "wisdom" literature. Did you know that Billy Graham reads through the books of Psalms and Proverbs every month? He's done it for almost fifty years! He says it's the one thing that has kept him on track in his relationships. Why not try this method yourself?

#2: The Word of Knowledge

How is the word of knowledge (*logos gnoseos* in the Greek) different from the word of wisdom? The word of knowledge is specific to a situation. It's when God suddenly reveals a practical solution to a specific problem.

For instance, let's say you're talking with someone who's having serious problems. You really don't know the person—you've never met him or her before that night. As you listen, seemingly out of nowhere, God gives you a specific, detailed, practical solution to that person's problem. But here's the catch— the person hasn't revealed to you the problem you have the solution to! But yet when you mention the solution to them, that person turns white and says, "How could you have known that?" That's the word of knowledge gift in operation.

#3: The Gift of Faith

As you examine this gift, you need to realize that the gift of faith is not the same thing as what theologians call "saving faith."

The idea of that Greek word for "saving faith" is "trust." Saving faith means you've come to the point where you no longer trust your religion, your goodness, your honest efforts to do right. You're relying solely on Jesus Christ and His death and resurrection for salvation. Everyone who becomes a Christian has saving faith.

But the gift of faith is different. It's literally the ability to believe God for specific results. What great power is present in that idea! But does that mean only certain Christians are able to believe God for results? Certainly not, because all of us are supposed to pray and trust God. But the gift of faith refers to those times and occasions when God has something very specific He wants to get done. As a result, He'll move in someone's heart who is willing to listen, who is willing to pray. As that person exercises the gift of faith, more of God's power is released. It's part of the way God works miracles. People who have the gift of faith believe so strongly that they expect God will act in a certain way, with a specific result.

#4: The Gifts of Healings

Because the Greek words are both in the plural, most grammarians believe that God gives gifts of being healed, not a gift of healing someone. Why do they think this? Because the plural carries the idea of God's distributing of something. That means that the Bible teaches that the gifts of healing are widely available. Although we don't have the power to heal anyone—only Jesus can do that—we can be a channel of faith, a channel of prayer. I believe that these gifts of healing are available to every Christian—they're not exclusive to a certain man or woman who is gifted with healing people.

But just because the gifts of healing are listed in the Bible, does that mean everybody will always be healed? I personally don't think so, and I'll tell you why. There are many passages in the Bible when God chooses for His own wisdom and purpose not to heal, when God allows difficult situations in order to help us mature as Christians.

Does that mean you shouldn't pray for healing? Of course not! The Bible says that if you're sick, pray for healing (James 5:14-15). But that doesn't mean you can depend on God for good health if you violate the laws of good health. If you abuse your body by not getting adequate exercise, fresh air, and good food, you can ask God for healing every day, but you will probably still have a body breakdown. You're violating the commonsense health principles God put into effect.

What's important to remember about healing is that God is not obligated to heal. You don't corner Him and insist He has to heal in this particular case. He chooses at times to heal and chooses at other times not to heal. In both cases, we need to have faith.

#5: The Working of Miracles

This gift means just what it says: the working of miracles. Some Bible scholars, however, believe it has to do with demonic deliverance. In other words, this gift refers to casting out demons in the name of Jesus.

#6: The Gift of Prophecy

Prophecy means to preach, tell forth, or communicate the message of God. Though most people associate this word with predicting the future, it typically has little to do with that. The root meaning of the word is "to tell God's message to people." When people are preaching God's message, it's powerful, and you know it. But God, talking to you right here, right now—that's the gift of prophecy in operation. It doesn't mean that the message will preclude or prohibit telling the future—just that the future is not the preeminent idea shared. For instance, the Old Testament prophets Jeremiah and Isaiah were given lots of messages. Although they were given predictive messages regarding the future, those messages were not primary. Instead, the messages of warning and repentance were what was important.

#7: Discernment of Spirits

The very term *discernment of spirits* implies there are different spirits. Today, movies that deal with sorcery, mediums, fortune-telling, and contacting dead spirits are proliferating. But the Bible warns us to stay away from such things (see Leviticus 19–20). We are to have nothing to do with divination—anything such as astrology, horoscopes, Ouija boards, mediums, spiritism—the whole works, because there is a curse on that kind of activity. Even the signs of the zodiac are trouble because the astrological star chart was originally developed by the Babylonians as a basis for demon worship. They believed the stars represented demons. And so I tell Christians, "Get that stuff out of your house!" After all, what's more important—what sign you're under or that God is Lord of your life?

The gift of discernment literally means "to see between," to understand whether or not something is really from God. This gift is so needed today in our mixed-up culture. You need to discern everything you read, examine, and do. Besides agreeing or disagreeing intellectually, you should sense spiritually whether something's right or not. Even if you don't have the actual spiritual gift of discernment, you can and should nurture your own skills of discernment.

How can you develop those skills? As you ever increase your detailed knowledge of the Bible, the Holy Spirit will help you. The more Scripture you know, the more error you will be able to identify.

#8: The Gift of *Genae Glosson*

Gene means various, and *glosson* means languages, so literally, it's the gift of tongues. But what does that mean? It refers to the God-given ability to speak in unknown languages. First Corinthians 12 mentions this gift, and so does Acts 2, but I believe these are essentially different gifts. There are eleven major differences between the gift of tongues in Acts and the gift of tongues in 1 Corinthians. The primary difference is that tongues in Acts were from known languages. In Acts 2:7-8, the text says, "These people are all from Galilee, and yet we hear them speaking the languages of the lands where we were born!" In other words, I believe that the gift of tongues in Acts is an evangelism gift, a demonstration that the message of Jesus is for everybody. But the passage in Corinthians indicates that the tongues are unknown, a prayer language that's a gift from God. This prayer language is a wonderful, vital, legitimate gift of God. I believe it's the way to pray that leads to more intimate communication with God. However, I personally don't believe this prayer language is a gift that every Christian has to experience. I believe you need to be filled with the Holy Spirit. But God will manifest different gifts in our lives.

The gift of tongues is a great gift. You cannot take a pair of spiritual scissors, cut out this gift, and eliminate it because you may not like it. It's as much a gift as prophecy and preaching. The New Testament model shows that for a church to be healthy and function properly, all of the gifts should be in balance, in order, and in operation. That's how the church gets its job done.

#9: Interpretation of Languages

It's intriguing that this one is listed immediately after the gifts of languages. That also makes it different from the book of Acts, where no one needed to interpret because they were speaking known languages.

But when a language is unknown, interpretation is needed. Scripture further points out that when unknown tongues are expressed in a public assembly, there should be an interpretation—otherwise the gift shouldn't be exercised (1 Corinthians 14:27-28). If you want to experience a prayer language, ask God for it. If God chooses to give it, wonderful. If He chooses not to give it to you, then ask Him to give you some other gift.

#10: The Gift of Teaching

This gift may coexist with preaching—or not. It's also mentioned in the fourth chapter of Ephesians. Basically, this gift involves an ability to explain spiritual truths clearly and accurately.

#11: The Gift of Helps

In trying to explain what this means, I've coined a phrase that I think is helpful—it's a gift of God to "fill the gaps." In other words, people with this gift realize what needs to be done in order for a function or ministry to operate properly. They have a special sensitivity to find out where that gap is—and to fill it.

#12: The Gift of Administration

In Greek, the word is *kuberneseis*, meaning "a person who is given the gift of a pilot." A gifted administrator is able to navigate between rocks and reefs to safely guide the ship into the harbor. That person has the gift of vision and the know-how to organize and accomplish a task.

#13: The Gift of Service

This gift is similar to the gift of helps. Some of the ways people excercise this gift are by feeding people and caring for them.

#14: The Gift of Encouragement

This gift in Romans 12:8, in the Greek, is *paraklesis* (similar to the Greek word used for the Comforter, the Holy Spirit—the *paraclete*), meaning "to come alongside." A person with this gift is good at comforting others, pouring courage into them— a gift greatly needed in this generation.

#15: The Gift of Giving

In Romans 12:8, this gift is translated as contributing to the needs of other people: "If you have money, share it generously." Although the word has a strong material root—meaning "give money"—it can also mean more than that. The Greek word translated *generously* can also mean "with sincerity." In other words, give without an ulterior motive—freely, generously, simply. So when you give, you're not doing it to control someone or inflate your ego. You're giving simply because you want to do it!

#16: Leadership

Taking the lead. Sound simple? Well, the Bible has something very specific to say about the kind of leadership God honors. Listen to these verses from 1 Timothy 3:1-5, for starters:

> *It is a true saying that if someone wants to be an elder, he desires an honorable responsibility. For an elder must be a man whose life cannot be spoken against. He must be faithful to his wife. He must exhibit self-control, live wisely, and have a good reputation. He must enjoy having guests in his home and must be able to teach. He must not be a heavy drinker or be violent. He must be gentle, peace loving, and not one who loves money. He must manage his own family well, with*

children who respect and obey him. For if a man cannot manage his own household, how can he take care of God's church?

In the Bible, leadership is not a position of privilege; it's a position of responsibility. It means being the example, taking the lead in being self-controlled, respectable, and honest.

#17: The Gift of Mercy

Although it's true that every Christian should show love, mercy, and compassion to people (see John 13:35), there are special gifts of mercy and compassion that are more intense and more focused.

Those who have the gift of mercy don't show it in such a smug, uppity, superior way that makes others feel ashamed. Instead, the gift of mercy means you lovingly build up others, giving them the help they need.

#18: The Gift of Evangelism

In Ephesians 4:11, the Greek word for evangelism means, technically, "explaining the gospel." In other words, a person with this gift is able to tell others about the good news of Jesus Christ clearly and succinctly.

A Last Word about Gifts

As soon as you start talking about spiritual gifts, people in the church get nervous. Why is that? Because even Christians disagree over spiritual gifts.

Here's one example. A few years ago I was invited to speak at a church in Indiana. The pastor was wonderful—a terrific young man and a talented public speaker. His church had begun to grow phenomenally and then hit a serious snag. So he asked me to come in and do a spiritual-growth conference. After speaking there all week, I became aware of the negative attitudes in the church. The people were so divided over one of the spiritual gifts that they sat on different sides of the church!

Then one night a miracle happened. At the conclusion of the service, a man in his mid-seventies who'd been a founder of the church and a key figure for over fifty years stood up. Because of a stroke, he was partially paralyzed and moved with great difficulty. But he literally dragged himself to the front of the church—and then burst into tears. He addressed the congregation, admitting that he'd had terrible bitterness toward someone in the church. On his way back down the aisle, he stopped beside a man in his thirties, who looked pale. The elderly man said, "I've hated you bitterly for years, and my hate has destroyed this church. Will you forgive me?"

I wonder if you can guess why that elderly man hated that young man? To quote his own words, "Because that young man spoke in tongues, and he and his charismatic friends talked about the gifts of the Holy Spirit. They said we needed more of the work of the Holy

57

Spirit in our church. I tried every way in my power to get that man to leave our church, but he wouldn't." As those men began to forgive one another, the Holy Spirit began to increase His dramatic activity in that congregation. And two or three years after that incident, the church experienced enormous spiritual growth.

Why did I tell you that story? Because I believe the devil has tricked so many Christians into fighting over something fundamental: the work of the Holy Spirit. Why would he do that? So we're divided in communicating the good news of the gospel of Jesus Christ. Instead, we need to be unified.

Whenever you're discussing spiritual gifts with others, remember that we, as Christians, are not here merely to debate doctrine or to win or lose arguments. We're here to fulfill our hunger for God's Spirit to work within each of us.

CHAPTER SIX

Learning about Prayer

When you think of prayer, what comes to mind? A bunch of high-sounding words? Getting on your knees by your bed? Folding your hands and saying "grace" at the table?

What is prayer really? It's simply communication—a two-way conversation—with God. And it's a major part of developing a spiritual root system. In this chapter, we'll look at why and when you should pray, how you can develop an attitude of prayer, the four elements of a prayer, some ideas for prayer starters, the types of prayer, and how to know when God is talking to you.

WHY SHOULD YOU PRAY?

Why is prayer so important? Here are eight good reasons.

#1: It's our communication link to God and His Son, Jesus Christ.

Jesus Himself said, in John 14:6, "I am the way, the truth, and the life. No one can come to the Father except through me." Because the Son is the doorway to God, you cannot know God unless you know Him through Christ and His death on the cross for you. Prayer allows a Christian direct access to God the Father through Jesus, our Savior.

When you learn how to pray, you are talking with the most powerful Being in the universe. The act of praying to an all-powerful God who loves you personally will open your eyes to both the beauty and the needs around you.

#2: It brings healing.

Being in God's presence through prayer brings the wonderful, healing peace of God to your heart—a quiet security in the Lord God Almighty. The apostle Paul writes:

> *Don't worry about anything; instead, pray about everything. Tell God what you need, and thank him for all he has done. If you do this, you will experience God's peace, which is far more wonderful than the human mind can understand. His peace will guard your hearts and minds as you live in Christ Jesus.* PHILIPPIANS 4:6-7

Since prayer brings healing, I encourage people who are in relationships to pray together. This works especially well when you're angry with each other, because prayer brings an inner quietness. Then it's hard to stay mad!

Awhile back, when my wife, Amy, and I

neglected praying together, we discovered that little frictions started wearing us down. But when we began to pray together again, God softened the friction areas. Truly a healing, humbling gentleness occurred when we prayed.

#3: It fixes your focus on God.

Why is that important? All of us can become so distracted by life's details and problems that we take our focus off God—the only one who can really help us.

Here's an example of a distracted prayer: "Lord, help me with my finances. We don't have money for the mortgage payment." The person stops praying. *Oh no,* he thinks, *what am I going to do?* "Lord, we need"—*What am I going to do?* "Lord, please"—*What AM I going to do? I don't have the money. Oh, good grief! Maybe if I took this money, maybe if I borrowed on this credit card, maybe if I . . .*

Do you see what's happening in that prayer? The person is starting to calculate the solution . . . and isn't praying anymore!

Real prayer fixes your focus on the source of your solution—God Himself. That's why it's vital for you to concentrate on who He is. If you learn how to pray effectively, your focus will be fixed on God, and *He* can give you solutions.

#4: It cultivates spiritual instincts.

When you have a daily time of wonderful, effective prayer, you'll learn to develop an instinct for what is of God and what is not. For example, as you're sitting in a meeting or watching something on TV, you'll sense an uneasiness in your spirit if what you're involved in isn't of God. James 4:8 makes the solution clear: "Draw close to God, and God will draw close to you."

A life of prayer doesn't mean you'll always be right, but it does mean you'll develop spiritual sensitivity.

#5: It cultivates an awareness of God's presence in your life.

If you're a Christian, God is with you right now. But you need to develop an awareness of His presence. The more you pray, the more God's presence will become real to you. Psalm 145:18 says, "The Lord is close to all who call on him, yes, to all who call on him sincerely."

One time I got into serious trouble in my own prayer life when I had a certain series of prayer experiences where God was so vividly real that I kept trying to duplicate the same feeling. Then, for about three months, I couldn't feel anything. I believe God withdrew those feelings from me on purpose because He wants us to operate on *faith,* not emotions. You can't manufacture God's presence. It comes naturally as you concentrate on loving Him, worshiping Him, and leading others to Him.

#6: It invokes God's protection.

As you communicate with God, He sends you help when you need it. Psalm 91:9-11 says:

> *If you make the Lord your refuge, if you make the Most High your shelter, no evil will conquer you; no plague will come near your dwelling. For he orders his angels to protect you wherever you go.*

#7: It's need-merging.

As you pray, you'll find that other people's needs come into your heart. You'll feel their hurt, their pain. You'll become more aware of how they need God's help. Then you'll be eager to pray for them and help them.

In Jeremiah 33:3, God says, "Ask me and I will tell you some remarkable secrets about what is going to happen here." As you "need-merge" in prayer, you can become a part of what God is doing all over the world. For instance, God may put a burden on your heart to pray for someone in China. As you pray for that person, who may be dealing with a difficult problem, you suddenly have worldwide influence!

Does that mean every time you pray God automatically answers the way you want Him to? No, it doesn't. God is still God, and He still has His purposes. But you can be a part of that purpose as you pray.

#8: It wins battles.

You can batter your battles with psychology.
You can hammer them with positive attitudes. You can smash them with hard work.
But they won't improve—until you pray.
James 5:16 says, "The earnest prayer of a
righteous person has great power and
wonderful results."

One of the greatest passages in the Bible on
prayer is in the book of Daniel. When Daniel
prayed, he got in trouble—in fact, he got thrown
into the lion's den. But he never stopped praying.
It was his lifeblood. This following passage,
Daniel 9:20-23, contains some thrilling, provoca-
tive, incredible statements about prayer.

> *I went on praying and confessing my sin
> and the sins of my people, pleading with
> the Lord my God for Jerusalem, his holy
> mountain. As I was praying, Gabriel,
> whom I had seen in the earlier vision, came
> swiftly to me at the time of the evening
> sacrifice. He explained to me, "Daniel, I
> have come here to give you insight and
> understanding. The moment you began
> praying, a command was given. I am here
> to tell you what it was, for God loves you
> very much. Now listen, so you can under-
> stand the meaning of your vision."*

When Daniel prayed, God responded by
sending angels into battle. What an awesome
responsibility!

If you ever want to know how important prayer is, read chapters 10 and 11 of Daniel. They give us a glimpse into a spiritual battle, as if God has suddenly ripped a curtain aside. In fact, this passage helps to answer the question, "When you pray for something and give it to God, can you stop praying?" As long as the burden is still there, keep praying. Why? Because you're empowering the angels to fight for you. As Daniel 10:12 says, "Don't be afraid, Daniel. Since the first day you began to pray for understanding and to humble yourself before your God, your request has been heard in heaven. I have come in answer to your prayer."

But sometimes finishing the battle takes time. Verse 13 says: "But for twenty-one days the spirit prince of the kingdom of Persia blocked my way. Then Michael, one of the archangels, came to help me, and I left him there with the spirit prince of the kingdom of Persia."

Because the battle against spirit princes or demons is mighty, we're all needed in the battle. Prayer is an urgent priority because Satan is trying to wreck everything Christians are doing. But we can help to guard these efforts with prayer—and send angels into battle.

Why doesn't God do this on His own? Because God's chosen us to be His allies. He's chosen to work in answer to prayer. He wants our involvement. And that's why we can't afford to neglect prayer. It has to be the first thing we do, not the last. Everything else flows from that.

Powerful benefits result from prayer: You communicate directly with God Himself, you experience healing, your focus becomes fixed on God, you develop spiritual instincts, you experience the presence of God more fully, you're protected from evil, you learn to pray for the needs of others, and you're more prepared for life's battles—seen and unseen. That's why prayer is so crucial.

WHEN SHOULD YOU PRAY?

How do you know when you should pray? Here are five great tips that help me.

Tip #1: Pray constantly and regularly. God's Word gives many examples of faithful people who led lives of prayer, and we're told to do the same. Ephesians 6:18 says, "Pray at all times and on every occasion in the power of the Holy Spirit. Stay alert and be persistent in your prayers for all Christians everywhere."

Pray every day, whether you feel like it or not. Even when you don't feel like it, you cannot afford to fail to pray. Why? Because that's when you need it the most. That feeling of apathy is like a red flag waving in front of your face!

Prayer takes discipline. It needs to be a regular commitment.

Tip #2: Pray anytime.

There is no "wrong" time to pray. The Bible is full of examples of praying in the morning, during the day, and at night. In 2 Timothy 1:3, the apostle Paul writes, "Night and day I constantly remember you in my prayers."

The important thing is that your prayer life fit your lifestyle and that you actually *pray*. Even if you are not a morning person (I'm not), start your day with some contact and worship of God—even if it's only for a few minutes. You need that focus for your day. But then make sure that your longer time of stopping, listening, taking notes, and praying is at the time of day that works with your lifestyle and personality. Some people have their concentrated prayer time late at night, others in the morning. I do a little of both. I start off in the morning, then have a longer time later at night, when I'm more alert.

Tip #3: Pray when you want to ask God for something.

Has there been any time this week when you really needed something? Even a little something? That's a time when you should pray. Nothing is too little, too selfish, or too embarrassing to take to your heavenly Father. After all, you're His child through your relationship with Jesus Christ and what Jesus did for you on the cross. In Matthew 6:9 and 11, Jesus models a daily-needs prayer for us: "Our Father in heaven, may your name be honored. . . . Give us our food for today."

When you're in trouble or are afraid, pray. In Psalm 91:15 the Lord says, "When they call on me, I will answer; I will be with them in trouble. I will rescue them and honor them." So when you're troubled, go to God. Focus on Him. Get His answer, His security, His help, and His power.

When you need wisdom about a decision, pray. Psalm 119:33-34 says, "Teach me, O Lord, to follow every one of your principles. Give me understanding and I will obey your law; I will put it into practice with all my heart." As a follower of God, you have access to the wisest Being in the universe. Go to Him with your problems, and He'll give you insight and wisdom.

You should also pray that God will show you the sin in your life. Psalm 139:23-24 says, "Search me, O God, and know my heart; test me and know my thoughts. Point out anything in me that offends you, and lead me along the path of everlasting life." When you start praying this way, God will show you areas where you are straying from His plan. As you draw closer to Him, your spiritual life will be revitalized.

Tip #4: Pray to rejoice in what God has given you.

Every one of us has much to be thankful for, even when we don't see things that way: life, a family, food, a place to live. So acknowledge the gifts God's given you. Praise and thank Him for them. Colossians 1:11-12 says, "May you be filled with joy, always thanking the Father, who has enabled you to share the inheritance that belongs to God's holy people, who live in the light."

Tip #5: Pray for the sheer pleasure of fellowshiping with God.

Talking with our Father should fill us with great joy. As Isaiah 56:7 says, "I will bring them also to my holy mountain of Jerusalem and will fill them with joy in my house of prayer. I will accept their burnt offerings and sacrifices, because my Temple will be called a house of prayer for all nations."

DEVELOPING AN ATTITUDE OF PRAYER

Now that you know why and when you should pray, how do you handle the times when you don't feel like it?

Here are six suggestions to help you develop a lifelong attitude of prayer.

#1: Lose your rebellion.

This may be a hard one to start off with, but if you come to God with a stubborn, rebellious heart, two things will happen: You'll be miserable, and God will be grieved. If you have unconfessed sin in your heart, take the caution of Psalm 66:18 to heart: "If I had not confessed the sin in my heart, my Lord would not have listened." So don't let your stubbornness get in the way of a wonderful relationship with God. After you confess your sins to God, He'll listen to your prayer, and your ears will be opened to His guidance.

#2: Listen to God.

Sometimes we simply need to keep quiet before God. The great evangelist D. L. Moody said, "Prayer is talking to God. The Bible is God talking to you. And it's best to let God do most of the talking!"

E. Stanley Jones, one of the great missionary leaders of the twentieth century, told me before his death that every morning he went to his "listening post." Once there, he'd sit down with a Bible, notebook, and pen and take an hour to listen quietly for God's guidance. But he didn't listen to every voice that floated through his mind. He'd write things down and then test them against the Bible. He said that the most wonderful experiences and the greatest knowledge in his life came from those listening times.

So why not keep a prayer journal like my wife, Amy, does? She continually writes down things she prays for and then dates and records God's answers. It's a journal of adventurous faith!

#3: Let your prayer life develop naturally. Don't feel pressured to learn how to pray. There is no "prayer saint," because prayer is a continual process. Yes, you must persist and hunger for time with God, but learn to let it grow naturally. Enjoy your times of prayer. Get excited about them. Grow with them. As Deuteronomy 4:29 says, "If you search for him with all your heart and soul, you will find him."

#4: Be God-centered not self-centered. Prayer can be therapeutic, but it's not therapy. Prayer should always be God-centered— not human-centered. You are there to worship, love, and praise Him. Psalm 17:1 says, "O Lord, hear my plea for justice. Listen to my cry for help. Pay attention to my prayer, for it comes from an honest heart."

#5: Be worship-driven. Love God. Enjoy Him. Praise Him. Honor Him. Laugh with Him. Spend time with Him. Talk to Him: "Lord, you're so wonderful. It's amazing how you brought me through that situation last week. I want to thank you again for it. I'm open to anything you want to teach me."

As Colossians 3:1-2 says,

> *Since you have been raised to new life with Christ, set your sights on the realities of heaven, where Christ sits at God's right hand in the place of honor and power. Let heaven fill your thoughts. Do not think only about things down here on earth.*

#6: Leave room for God to be God.
For all of its power, prayer is not your telling God what to do. Prayer is not your manipulating God. Some people pray for healing or pray for help, but they don't get what they pray for. Does that mean their faith is defective? No. God does things in ways we don't understand. He may have other, bigger purposes in mind.

God has a purpose for your life, and He has worked out everything that will affect that purpose. For example, what if you get sick this week and pray, asking God to heal you? What if God, in His sovereignty, wants you to meet a doctor, for the purpose of leading him to Christ, during your process of being ill?

We must remember that we don't know the whole picture, but God does. That's why we need to pray within the parameters of His will. It's not a "wimp out" to pray, *Lord, please do this for me if it's in Your will.* That's biblical. But verses such as Matthew 21:22, which says, "If you believe, you will receive whatever you ask for in prayer," can sometimes throw

72

people off. This verse isn't saying you can have anything you want. It means that God will grant your request if it fits His purpose for your life and if you're praying in compatibility with God's purpose for your life.

If God gave us everything we asked for, we'd be in trouble. Our lives would be wrecked. For example, if God had given me the wife I'd asked for when I was a teenager, it would have been a total mistake. That woman was the wrong person for me. Because we're limited in our maturity and knowledge, we need to remember that God always knows what's best for us. And He can see the whole picture.

The Four Elements of Prayer

If you're not sure what you should say when you pray, ACTS can help. This acrostic stands for four different elements of talking with God:

A = Adoration—praising God
C = Confessing your sins to God and asking for forgiveness
T = Thanking God for all He's done for you
S = Supplication—asking God for help

A=Adoration
The first element of prayer is praising God. So worship Him. Express your heart. Show your love for Him.

In the book of Psalms in the Old Testament, a phrase is repeated frequently: "Bless the Lord." Psalm 103:1 says, "Bless the Lord, O my soul; And all that is within me, bless His holy name!" (NKJV). It's easy to understand God's blessing of us, but how can we bless God?

In the Hebrew language, blessing the Lord means expressing your adoration of Him, your thanks, your gratefulness. Try singing (out loud or to yourself) a praise song or hymn.

C=Confession

Second, you need to confess your sins (some Christians call them *sins of commission*) to God and ask for His forgiveness. You may think, *I don't have anything to confess—I'm kind to my family, honest in my work, etc.* But sin can creep into your life without your even being aware of it. "Secret" sins like self-ishness, pride, jealousy, prejudice, and lust can slowly eat away at your soul and begin to destroy your relationships with God and others. Even the apostle Paul, the author of many of the epistles in the New Testament, wrote in 1 Timothy 1:15, "Christ Jesus came into the world to save sinners—and I was the worst of them all."

Another category of sin is called *sins of omission*. This type of sin is defined in James 4:17: "Remember, it is sin to know what you ought to do and then not do it." Have you ever felt as if God wanted you to talk to someone about Him, but you just blew it off? Or have you thought, *I should give money to that cause,* but then you forgot about it? Have you ever ignored someone you knew needed your encouragement? This type of sin needs to be confessed as well.

T=Thanking God

In the third part of prayer, we recognize how much God has given us: the gift of salvation, the forgiveness of our sins, our very lives, the beautiful world around us—everything! Hebrews 12:28 says, "Since we are receiving a Kingdom that cannot be destroyed, let us be thankful and please God by worshiping him with holy fear and awe." God delights in thankful hearts.

Thanking God is an important part of your relationship—even at times when it's difficult to be grateful. An extra bonus to practicing thankfulness in prayer is that it often affects your outlook as well. If you list ten things you can thank God for, you'll be amazed at how quickly your attitude will improve.

S=Supplication

Asking God to supply your needs is the fourth part of prayer. The Bible instructs us to ask God for specific help. In the Lord's Prayer in Matthew 6, Jesus models this element of prayer: "Give us our food for today" (verse

11). Throughout the Bible numerous people prayed to God for help, healing, solutions, protection, and spiritual growth. You, too, can ask God for needs to be met. As Philippians 4:6 states it, you can "tell God what you need, and thank him for all he has done."

Another element of supplication is *intercession,* praying for others. Family members, friends, pastors, business contacts, church members, and missionaries are all in need of our prayers. In 2 Thessalonians 1:11-12 the apostle Paul describes his use of intercessory prayer:

> *And so we keep on praying for you, that our God will make you worthy of the life to which he called you. And we pray that God, by his power, will fulfill all your good intentions and faithful deeds. Then everyone will give honor to the name of our Lord Jesus because of you, and you will be honored along with him. This is all made possible because of the undeserved favor of our God and Lord, Jesus Christ.*

Now that you know the four elements of prayer, how can you get started?

PRAYER STARTERS

If you struggle with getting into the right frame of mind to pray, here are six starters that I've found helpful in my own prayer life.

RON BALL

#1: Try praise.
If I'm having trouble praying, I start thanking God and praising him. Praise, worship, and thanksgiving can create a surge of prayer. Why? Because God delights in it, it's good for you, and the devil hates it. Praise—honoring and worshiping God—is a great way to start prayer.

#2: Listen to music.
The second way to kick start your prayer life is through great Christian music. I have a CD called *Celebrate* that puts me in a mood of wanting to be close to God.

I also use music in another way. I read words from hymns such as "Crown Him with many crowns, the Lamb upon His throne" and "Jesus loves me, this I know." When I worry about finances, I'll read, "A mighty fortress is our God, a bulwark never failing." The lyrics of the hymns are so incredible, so full of great theology and poetry that they make me want to pray.

#3: Read Scripture.
Another great prayer starter is the songbook of the Bible: the book of Psalms. Originally they were sung to music. I like praying from the Psalms even better than praying from hymnbooks because this prayer starter is actually the Word of God. Try reading a psalm such as 8:1: "O Lord, our Lord, the majesty of your name fills the earth!"

#4: Join others.

Outside support—praying with a friend, family member, or small group—is a good starter. In Matthew 18:19-20, Jesus says: "I also tell you this: If two of you agree down here on earth concerning anything you ask, my Father in heaven will do it for you. For where two or three gather together because they are mine, I am there among them."

#5: Move around.

Praying to God doesn't mean you always need to kneel down beside your bed. (In fact, that can lead me to fall asleep at times!) In 2 Samuel 7:18 the Bible says David "sat" before the Lord. First Kings 8:54 says Solomon raised his arms to God as he was kneeling, and then he stood. Physical movement can rejuvenate your prayer life.

#6: Vary your environment.

The Bible tells of many different places where people prayed: at home (Daniel 6:10), on a mountainside (Luke 6:12), on a shore (Acts 21:5), and even on a roof (Acts 10:9)!

So do something to vary your physical surroundings: take a walk outside, go to a different room in the house than where you normally pray, take a drive in your car, or walk up a mountain.

After you start your prayer, where do you go from there? You investigate different types of prayer.

Six Types of Prayer

You've probably heard all sorts of prayers—
ones that sound more formal, others that
sound more conversational. How do you
know if you're praying the right way?

Surprise! There isn't a right way. You
might want to try mixing and matching
the following types to see what works for
you.

Formal prayers

Formal prayers are written by someone else
and then read. An example could be found
in a source such as *The Book of Common
Prayer*. Although some people find formal
prayers too stilted and rigid for their
personal taste, they can be incredibly
powerful. What makes the difference is
whether the person reading it is really praying—or just mouthing mechanical, cold,
empty words.

Another important thing to check with
formal prayer is the content. Make sure it
squares against what the Bible says.

Conversational prayers

Conversational prayer means that you talk to
God as if you're talking to a friend. You
don't have to use religious language, flowery
phrases, or "thee" and "thou" to impress
God. He just wants to communicate with
you from the heart.

Silent prayers

Prayer doesn't always have to be out loud. Sometimes it's without words—it's private, taking place in the quiet of your heart.

Snatch prayers

This kind of prayer is done on the run, in a hurry. You just "snatch" a quick prayer moment, such as, *Lord, give me wisdom about what I should say to this person.*

Are snatch prayers irreverent? No, as long as you mean them. What makes something irreverent toward God is a bad attitude.

Letter prayers

If you communicate and express yourself better by words on paper than you do verbally, write God a letter: *Dear Jesus, I want to talk to you about this problem* or *I want to thank you for . . .* Open your heart to God in your letter, and then sign and date it.

Pervasive prayers

Pervasive prayer means prayer that merges into your life all the time. It's in and out, but it's always there. It means that you'll pray when something comes up, be it in the grocery store, at the office, or in the car.

Sometimes we overorganize prayer. But it should be natural, like breathing air. The most important thing is to communicate with your loving Creator, God.

HOW TO KNOW IF GOD SPEAKS TO YOU

If someone told you, "I hear voices," what would you think of that person? Many of you would probably think, *You're nuts! You should undergo psychiatric evaluation.* And sometimes you'd be right.

But when it comes to hearing the voice of God, that's an entirely different matter. Most of the time God communicates with us through the Bible. For instance, 2 Timothy 3:16 says, "All Scripture is inspired by God and is useful to teach us what is true and to make us realize what is wrong in our lives. It straightens us out and teaches us to do what is right." Other times God will communicate to us through mental images and pictures. He'll impress a thought or idea on your mind, and you'll know it's from God. However, if God wants to communicate verbally and audibly with you, that's His business. First Kings 19:12 describes God's voice as a "gentle whisper."

How do you know it's God's voice—and not your own or the devil's—speaking to you? There are two basic answers to that question.

Answer #1: Test it with these five steps.

1. Test it against the Bible. God is not going to tell you to do anything that contradicts or violates His written Word.
2. Test it by talking to godly people. If you're

unsure of the Bible's teaching and you believe God is telling you something, talk about it with godly friends who love the Lord.

3. Test it by opening or closing doors to confirm God's message.

4. Test it by the inner peace that you feel. Does peace grow in your heart or go away? Does a sense of rightness grow or a sense of discomfort?

5. Test it by reason and intelligence.

Answer #2: Take it through the humility test. I believe you can test the voice you hear in prayer by approaching it with personal humility. If a person passes a message to you from God, is that person being truly humble? Do they say, "You know, I may be wrong, and I'm not telling you what to do, but when I prayed for you the other day, I really felt . . ."?

Having a humble spirit is so important because we, as humans, can be wrong sometimes. And that humility will protect you from believing something (such as God intended me to marry this person . . .) just because you *want* to believe it.

As you test God's voice, you'll learn more about Him. And as you grow closer to Him in fellowship, your spiritual insights will become more focused and targeted. Then you'll be able to tell when it's God—or yourself, others, or the devil—talking.

Learning to pray is one of the most important things you can do to help yourself grow spiritually. I know, because it's made a tremendous difference in my own spiritual growth.

When I was thirteen, a man explained to me, with great simplicity, what knowing Jesus was all about. It wasn't about religion or being baptized; it wasn't about being a good person; it was about my realizing that I'd sinned against God by being selfish and trying to run my own life. He told me that my only hope was to ask Christ to come into my life and forgive me. When I accepted Christ's sacrifice for me, God changed my attitudes and my inner heart.

But for the next two years I had no further training, and I floundered in my faith. I realized that if I was ever going to be what God wanted me to be, something had to change dramatically. So I went to the pastor of my church and asked if he'd trust me with a key to the building so I could have a place to pray every day. He considered my request and then gave me a key. Every day after school, I walked the mile and a half to the church. I was committed to praying an hour each day.

The first day I felt uneasy as I walked into the dark sanctuary. But, determined, I knelt down at the altar and repeated every fancy prayer I could remember. I prayed and prayed until I was almost certain that forty-five or fifty minutes had passed. When I glanced at my watch, I couldn't believe it! I had only been there five minutes! The time crept by, and I was close to giving up. But something inside me (later I realized it was the Spirit of God Himself communicating to my spirit) said, *You can't quit. This is the key to knowing Me.*

So I stuck with it. A week, two weeks, a month, three months finally passed. At the end of those three months, a whole spiritual dimension began to open up. I discovered that prayer is actually communicating with God. I began to sense solutions to problems. My perspective, my view of the world was radically altered.

Yours can be, too.

CHAPTER SEVEN

Studying Your Bible

In the last chapter, we talked about prayer as two-way communication between you and God. But God also communicates in another way—through His inspired Word. He speaks directly to you through Scripture.

Do you get intimidated just thinking about reading the Bible? After all, it's a pretty hefty book with lots of pages and tiny print. Do you wonder if you need a seminary degree to understand it?

Well, you don't. The Bible was written so that all could understand it. For instance, the apostle Paul wrote the book of 2 Timothy to a young man who was a kind of protégé of his. And here's what Paul told Timothy about the importance of studying the Bible:

> *You have been taught the holy Scriptures from childhood, and they have given you the wisdom to receive the salvation that comes by trusting Christ Jesus. All Scripture is inspired by God and is useful to teach us what is true and to make us realize what is wrong in our lives. It*

85

> *straightens us out and teaches us to do*
> *what is right. It is God's way of preparing*
> *us in every way, fully equipped for every*
> *good thing God wants us to do.*
>
> 2 TIMOTHY 3:15-17

The Bible is not just a collection of religious sayings or an ancient manuscript from another culture. It isn't simply a human book. It's the inspired Word of God, His chosen communication with the human race. The Bible, from Genesis to Revelation, is without error. There is not a mistake or a contradiction anywhere within its pages. It's God's blueprint for life.

When you spend time reading the Bible, you're dealing with the Creator of the universe. You're dealing with the God who made your amazing body, who created your brainpower.

Don't you want to know what that God thinks? Don't you want to discover what His plan is for the human race? Don't you want to live forever? Someday all of us are going to meet God. And, depending on whether or not you decide to believe that Jesus is God's Son, who died on the cross for your sins, you'll live forever in heaven or hell. The Bible is the manual that points the way toward knowing God and eternal life with Him.

And since the Bible is your main source for learning about God (since Jesus no longer walks the earth today in human form), you need to remember that you have a vicious enemy, Satan, who opposes every step of your spiritual growth. He wants to make you lazy. He wants to keep you unaware of what spiritual growth can mean in your life. He wants to get rid of the power you can have from walking with God.

How could the devil accomplish this? One way is by turning you away from from studying the Bible. Here are Satan's top three myths to keep you away from the most powerful, life-changing book you could ever read.

Myths about the Bible

Myth #1: It's too hard to understand.
Do you think God would love you, want you to go to heaven, want you to be forgiven, and then give you a Bible you couldn't understand? God cares more about you than to give you a confusing message. He wants you to study and know His Word.

It's true that the Bible has such great depth and power that you could spend the rest of your life studying it and never learn all that it teaches. But it's also so simple that the most uneducated person can delve into its contents, get to know God better, and learn how to live successfully. The only catch about finding the life principles of the Bible is that you have to be willing to look for them.

Myth #2: It's boring and dull.
On the contrary! There's more human
drama, emotion, and flesh-and-blood living
in the Bible than in ten episodes of *The X-
Files, Melrose Place,* and *As the World Turns*
put together. Love, murder, sacrifice, adultery, prophecies, jealousy, political strife,
intrigue—it's all there. And even more exciting is that throughout the Old and New
Testaments you're told how God can release
power in *your* life. It's an awesome book!

Myth #3: You're too busy.
Have you ever thought, *Why should I take
time to read an ancient document? My time
is too precious!*

Well, if you think that, in a way you're
actually saying that you don't have time for
God. You don't have time to learn how life
works from God's perspective. You don't have
time for truth. You don't have time to study
the book that will give you the best advice
possible for your relationships and situations.

But if you take time to study the Bible, it
will be well worth the moments you spend,
as this next section shows.

WHY MAKE IT A PRIORITY?

What are the results of putting Bible study as
a priority in your spiritual growth? You—
and your life—will change. Here are five
benefits you'll receive:

Benefit #1: Reminders

Bible study will remind you of your duties as a Christian and of how much God loves you. You'll also receive reminders of His power when you read about miracles, such as the parting of the Red Sea and Daniel in the lion's den, and reminders of who God is and why He sent His Son, Jesus Christ, to pay the price for our sins. Through your study of God's Word, you'll have incredible reminders of how God works in your life.

Benefit #2: Reference points

You'll develop "reference points" to understand what's going on in the world around you. When you see something questionable, you'll become more and more able to discern how God would view it, as you refer to Scripture you've studied. God will never tell you anything that contradicts the Bible, since it is His Word, an expression of His character.

Benefit #3: Reasons

The Bible will help you understand life better—why certain things happen to certain people in certain ways.

Although it's difficult to understand why some things happen (such as natural disasters, illness, or serious accidents), there are other areas of life where it's possible to know why things happen. For example, the following two verses give examples of why God won't answer your prayers. Psalm 66:18 says, "If I had not confessed the sin in my heart, my Lord would not have listened." First Peter 3:7 says, "If you [husband] don't treat her [your wife] as you should, your prayers will not be heard."

Benefit #4: Results

The best answer to the boredom of an endless, mediocre life is studying the Bible. Why? Because as you read and begin to follow the principles of the Bible, you'll see results in your relationships, your work, your attitudes, etc.

Benefit #5: Renewal

When you study the Bible, you'll be renewed in energy, spirit, faith, and strength. In addition, your ability to forgive people will be renewed the more the Word of God takes root in your life.

With these kind of results, how could you *not* want to study the Bible? So let's plunge in!

Practical Steps

Following are two specific, practical steps you can take.

Step #1: Be regular.

Make a commitment to study your Bible every day. Why is this so important? Because having a regular Bible study is a big part of developing a spiritual root system. You

cannot pull the nutrients from your root
system unless you are being fed by the Bible
on a consistent basis. Otherwise you'll begin
to starve spiritually.

But as much as you can try to read God's
Word every day, there will be days that you
miss. On such days, don't worry that God
will come down hard on you in fierce judgment. Such thoughts are of the devil, to
discourage you and make you feel guilty so
that you don't go back to studying the Bible.
So if you miss a day, pick it up the next day—
and enjoy that communication with your
Father.

Step #2: Get help.
There are five "helps," besides the Bible, that
I recommend:

■ A modern translation
Although many people are accustomed to the
King James Version, which was released in
1611 and revised in the 1700s, it's important
to remember that it's a translation (in other
words, someone's interpretation of the original Greek and Hebrew). In fact, for fifty years
after its release, people had to fight for it because
others only wanted the "real" translation
(at that time it was the Bishop's Bible, which
was prominently used in England). After this
initial struggle for acceptance the King James
Version gradually came to be respected,
loved, and appreciated for its beautiful

Elizabethan English and terminology that's found in great Shakespearean literature.

Why did I give a history lesson? For this purpose only: If you find your current Bible hard to understand, why not try a more modern translation? I recommend the New Living Translation, an excellent, accurate translation that is close to the Greek and Hebrew manuscripts. It's easy to read—and in modern English. The New International Version is also a good choice.

■ A basic Bible dictionary.
Go to a Christian bookstore and buy a basic Bible dictionary (*Smith's Bible Dictionary* is a good, simple one). Use it to look up words, places, customs, and biblical geography as you read through the Bible.

■ An inexpensive concordance
A concordance traces all the words in the Bible. For instance, if you're trying to think of a verse and can remember only one word, go to your concordance. It will list for you every Bible verse where the word is used. This is a great study tool, for you'll be able to cross-reference different verses on the same topic.

■ A notebook
In this notebook (use a different one than your prayer notebook), record:

1. Verses that are particularly helpful to you
2. A concept that leaps off the page and grips you
3. A phrase that gives you the help you need that day
4. A section of Scripture that puzzles you

As you're reading, write these things down in your notebook. Then, when you find the solution to a problem, write it down also and record the date.

■ A Bible study guide

There are numerous Bible studies and Bible study series—many of which are very good—available in Christian bookstores. One such line is the *Fisherman Bible Studyguides* (Harold Shaw Publishers), which are based on the inductive method: what the text says, what it means, how it applies to you. There are also several organizations, such as Bible Study Fellowship, Precept Ministries (Kay Arthur), and the Navigators, that carry Bible study programs. To show you how a study might work, let's take the Navigators' material as an example. In workbook format, the study states a question, gives you a portion of Scripture to look up, and then helps you figure out the answer. As you study, you become more grounded in God's Word—and in problem solving through His eyes.

METHODS OF STUDYING THE BIBLE

You may want try several different methods of studying the Bible to help you evaluate which one works best for you. Or, to keep your studying fresh, switch between the methods.

Entire Bible

If you're a new Christian or don't know very much about the Bible, I suggest you start your reading in the New Testament. That doesn't mean the Old Testament isn't valuable or important; you'll want to go back and read through the entire Old Testament later. But the New Testament provides a foundation for learning who Jesus is and the basics of Christian growth. Billy Graham recommends the Gospel of John as a great starting place.

If you'd like to read the whole Bible through, try one of these plans:

- First option: Read three chapters a day and five on Sunday. Start in Genesis and read through Revelation.
- Second option: Purchase *The One Year® Bible* (Tyndale House Publishers), which divides the Bible for you and includes both Old and New Testament readings for each day.

Either option takes about twenty to thirty minutes for an average reader. When you invest that amount of time each day, the

Bible's principles will produce greater success than you've ever dreamed possible in your heart, home, work, and relationships. It's an investment you cannot afford to miss.

Topical
A topical study means you pick a topic and study it. For example, let's say you wanted to do a study on love. First, you would find the word in your concordance and note all the references in the Bible on love. Then you would go to your Bible and read every verse on the topic. You would use your notebook to scribble comments and questions, until you've gone through every verse on that topic.

Biographical (also known as character)
To keep your study fresh, why not examine a Bible person? For example, what could you learn if you studied the life of King David in the Old Testament? He was powerful, wealthy, talented, and loved God, yet he also sinned greatly. As you study the characters of the Bible, you can see for yourself which life principles work—and which ones don't. David, Job, Abraham, Moses, Ruth, Deborah, Peter, Mary, Paul, and many more make for intriguing study.

Book
For this type of study, I suggest you start with a simpler, shorter book. For example, the book of Philippians has only four chapters. But it's

so full of joy and excitement it could get even a negative thinker to think positively. So sit down and read the whole book when you're discouraged. Then read it a second and a third time. And after you've read it through three times, go back—section by section, chapter by chapter—and use your notebook to help you dig into the meaning of the book, recording your questions in your notebook. If you don't know what a word or phrase means, look it up in your Bible dictionary. Studying a book will deepen your knowledge of God's message to the world—and to you.

Chapter

Pick a chapter and read it through three times. (You may want to try reading it in three different translations, because each translation may give you a new insight.) After you've read it through three times, pick what you think is the key verse of the chapter and write it down.

After you've picked a key verse, give the chapter a title. For example, if you're studying Psalm 23, you might title it "God's Plan of Protection" or "The Shepherd's Psalm." And don't worry—you don't have to impress anybody with your literary skills. The idea is to get into the Bible, so the Bible can get into you.

Memorizing Bible Verses

In order for the principles of the Bible to stay firmly implanted in your life, why not try memorizing a few verses? It's not as scary as it looks, and the advantages are threefold.

First, when you fill your mind and heart with the Word of God, you'll find yourself doing what it says, and that is always good. As James 1:25 states, "If you keep looking steadily into God's perfect law—the law that sets you free—and if you do what it says and don't forget what you heard, then God will bless you for doing it."

Second, when you are enduring tough times and are in a situation where you don't have a Bible with you, you can be inspired and comforted from meditating on Bible passages you've memorized.

Third, if you are telling someone about your faith in Jesus Christ, memorizing the verses that highlight the key points of salvation will help you as you talk to that person.

How do you memorize? The secret of memorization is repetition. If you repeat something often enough, you'll remember it. Some people like to write the verses they are memorizing on cards and post them in their car or kitchen or on the bathroom mirror as a constant reminder. Other people like to read their portion out loud several times each day. Whatever method you choose, the key to memorization is repetition. Even after you have a verse thoroughly memorized, continue to review it weekly so you don't forget.

If you'd like to memorize Scripture but

don't know where to start, here is a listing of verses I recommend for memory:

John 3:16
John 11:25
John 14:6
Ephesians 2:8-9
Philippians 2:13
Philippians 4:4
Philippians 4:6-8
Philippians 4:19
1 John 1:9
Isaiah 41:10, 13
Lamentations 3:22-23

In order for your spiritual root system to become healthy, it's paramount that you study God's Word. For as you debunk the myths about Bible reading, make your study a priority, learn different methods of investigating what Scripture says, and then memorize portions of passages to take with you, you are growing to be more like Christ.

CHAPTER EIGHT

Sharing Your Faith

Recently, while on an airplane, I sat next to a soldier. I tried several times to engage him in conversation, but he'd just mumble or give me one-word answers. Then he'd turn away again and grow quiet.

So after thinking for a few minutes, I decided to ask him about his family. The response was amazing. He came alive! In fact, he almost jumped out of his seat. He excitedly whipped out his wallet and pulled out a stack of pictures of his children (including his newest baby girl) and his wife. It was obvious the soldier loved his family and was proud of them.

What made the difference in the soldier's behavior? Why was he talking all of a sudden? He was motivated to talk because he had something he believed in. His family was a topic of love, excitement, and affection.

How exciting it would be if we felt that same way about Jesus Christ! Then we'd *want* to share his saving message with everyone around us. It would be a natural outflow of our life—out of gratitude for what Christ has done for us.

The thought of witnessing may sound intimidating (maybe we're afraid of open rejection or being laughed at), but it's not something we are given a choice about. Not only is witnessing a great way to grow spiritually, it's a command given to us by Jesus.

> *Therefore, go and make disciples of all the nations, baptizing them in the name of the Father and the Son and the Holy Spirit. Teach these new disciples to obey all the commands I have given you. And be sure of this: I am with you always, even to the end of the age.*
>
> MATTHEW 28:19-20

So why is sharing Christ with others so difficult sometimes? Maybe it's a problem of inflow, without outflow. Let me explain with this illustration. There's a body of water in Israel, known as the Dead Sea, that's almost stagnant. Anyone can float on it without sinking because of its high salt content. Why is the Dead Sea so dead? Because the Jordan River flows into it from the north, and no major tributary flows out of it from the south. It has inflow, but no outflow.

The same "outflow" problem can put your life in spiritual danger. It's great to study the Bible and have a meaningful prayer life. But if you keep God's love to yourself, you'll stagnate spiritually, wallowing in your own selfishness. God says that you need to share Jesus with others. So be a part of pointing others toward the experience of accepting God's love and eternal salvation.

God wants you to develop a heart of utter love, truthfulness, and compassion for people who don't yet know Christ. In Romans 9:1-3, Paul writes:

> *In the presence of Christ, I speak with utter truthfulness—I do not lie—and my conscience and the Holy Spirit confirm that what I am saying is true. My heart is filled with bitter sorrow and unending grief for my people, my Jewish brothers and sisters. I would be willing to be forever cursed—cut off from Christ!—if that would save them.*

Second Corinthians 5:10-11 also speaks of the attitude we should have about helping others spiritually:

> *For we must all stand before Christ to be judged. We will each receive whatever we deserve for the good or evil we have done in our bodies.*
>
> *It is because we know this solemn fear of the Lord that we work so hard to persuade others. God knows we are sincere, and I hope you know this, too.*

WHAT IS WITNESSING?

When you witness to someone, you need to talk with them on a personal level. And it's important you get across a fourfold message:

#1: Tell people about Jesus.

In order to do so, you need to be prepared. You need to have your facts straight. You need to understand who Jesus is. As the apostle Peter wrote:

> *You must worship Christ as Lord of your life. And if you are asked about your Christian hope, always be ready to explain it. But you must do this in a gentle and respectful way. Keep your conscience clear. Then if people speak evil against you, they will be ashamed when they see what a good life you live because you belong to Christ.* 1 PETER 3:15-16

You don't have to be a pastor or a missionary to communicate the Good News. A basic knowledge of the fundamentals of Christianity is all you need. If a friend or acquaintance asks you a question about Christianity that you don't know how to answer, say, "That's a good question—I'm not sure what the answer is. Let me find out for you." Then go to your pastor or a mature-in-the-faith Christian friend and find out what the answer is.

Telling people about Jesus doesn't require

special training. However, your confidence level will be strengthened if you spend some time studying the subject. Many people have found it helpful to keep a tract like *The Four Spiritual Laws* or some other gospel presentation in their Bible. In addition, most churches offer classes and seminars on sharing your faith.

Many people want to study Christianity on their own before making a decision to accept Jesus Christ, so make sure they have a Bible in a modern translation. Encourage them to begin their study of Christianity in the New Testament, in the book of John. Then, if they wish to read further, suggest they read Matthew, Mark, and Luke (the other three New Testament Gospels) as well. For other sources that may prove helpful in introducing them to Christ, see "Recommended Reading" on page 121.

#2: Share what Christ has done for you. The book of John tells the story about Jesus' healing of a man who was born blind. When the Jewish leaders who were trying to discredit Jesus asked the man what happened, the man replied, "I know this: I was blind, and now I can see!" (John 9:25). What a powerful statement of who Jesus really is!

So don't underestimate the strength of your personal testimony. In Acts 26, the apostle Paul gave his testimony to King Agrippa.

Although his testimony didn't cause Agrippa to accept Christ, it showed the king that Paul was not guilty of the crimes with which he'd been charged.

Although some will have a more dramatic testimony than others, never feel that your testimony isn't "exciting" enough to share. The peace, joy, and love that a relationship with Christ brings is an out-of-this-world experience—and everyone needs to know about Him.

#3: Communicate what Christ can do for them.

Let's say you meet a woman in a grocery store, and she begins to tell you about the problems with her rebellious teenage son. Because you've experienced the same kind of problem, you can say, "You know, I went through that, so I know how you feel. Sometimes I'd get so mad at him, I could spit. But since I've come to know Jesus Christ, He's helped me solve my problem. Do you want to know how?"

She'll probably say yes, if for no other reason than to be polite.

Then say, "He helped me by giving me more love for my son. He helped me because in the Bible I find wisdom for ways of dealing with him. . . ." Then list some practical things that you've done to help your son and to help yourself deal with him in a more positive manner. If she still looks interested, you could follow up with, "I always thought knowing God was going to church and being a do-gooder or being religious. I always thought it was just trying to balance my guilt against the good things and bad things I do."

Say next, "Jesus Christ can help you, too," and then give her a reason to know Jesus Christ: "I learned the truth: that I can be free! Because Jesus died for me on the cross, I can really know Him. Would you like to know Him, too?" If so, tell her, with great simplicity, how she could accept Christ.

Communicating how a relationship with Christ would affect them in the midst of a problem or situation is a terrific starting point for drawing people to the saving message of the gospel.

#4: Ask if they want to know Christ personally.

When the time seems appropriate, simply say, "Would you like me to pray with you? Would you like to ask Jesus to come into your life?"

If the person says no, back off kindly. But continue to show them Christlike love, respect their choice, and, wherever possible, build a bridge of friendship with them.

If the person says yes, then lead them in a prayer:

"Father in Heaven, I do believe that Jesus Christ is who He says He is and that He died for me. I fully and voluntarily turn away from my sins and the selfish control of my life. I invite Jesus Christ to come into my life as my only Lord and Savior. I do not depend on my goodness, my efforts, or my observance of religion. I depend only on what Jesus Christ did for me on the cross. I believe now that He has forgiven me, that He is my Savior and Lord, and that from this day forward I belong to Him and will live my life for Him. Thank You for hearing and answering this prayer. In Jesus' name, Amen."

THINGS TO REMEMBER WHEN WITNESSING

Talking to others about Christ isn't always easy. That's why it's good to keep these three important statements in mind so you won't become discouraged.

Reminder #1: Witnessing takes time and patience.

It would be great if every person you talked with immediately saw a need to follow Jesus. But that's not how a talk usually happens. Most conversions come as a result of a relationship built with another person, and relationships take time.

So when you're preparing to witness, consider every person who doesn't know Jesus as an island and yourself as the boat.

As you circle around and around the island,
looking for a place to land your boat, you
have trouble. The harbors are rocky and
exposed to the wind and the ocean. But as
you continually keep boating around that
island, you finally see one tiny piece of beach
where you can land.

That's the way it is with people. You may
need to circle, in friendship, a person's life
for a long time before you find a place where
he'll let you land, where she'll trust you. That
one little "beach" may be marriage troubles,
financial pressures, midlife crisis, or inner
emptiness. Although "circling the island"
could take years (and you may never see the
results in your lifetime), work hard to find
that one little piece of beach where that
person is vulnerable, and then land there.
The eternal results are worth the wait.

**Reminder #2: Witnessing isn't being
judgmental or winning arguments.**
All of us have known men and women who
have crusaded for their faith in a negative,
sour, and unpleasant way. They enjoy arguing
and fighting. They're cantankerous and
ornery. And unfortunately, because they're
trying so hard to get the last word, win the
argument, and prove they're right, they hurt
the name of Jesus. They fail because they're
trying to bully people into the kingdom of
God.

But a person who really loves Jesus will want others to know about Him. He'll communicate the message in love and with a spirit of help and encouragement. In 1 Thessalonians, Paul writes, "We loved you so much that we gave you not only God's Good News but our own lives, too" (1 Thessalonians 2:8).

Reminder #3: It's more than living a good life in front of people.

As I sat in the emergency room of a hospital, I started talking with a woman who claimed to be a Christian. But when I asked her how she told others about Jesus, she spouted this answer: "Well, I don't have to tell people about Jesus because I just live a wonderful Christian life in front of them." Later, another woman told me she'd just shared the gospel with one of her neighbors for the first time. The woman had lived in that neighborhood for six years and had always been a wonderful neighbor. But when she shared Jesus with her neighbor, who was very sick with cancer, her non-Christian neighbor said, "I never knew you were a Christian. I thought you were just a nice neighbor."

It's true that if you don't live consistently, you're wasting your breath, and you might as well keep your mouth shut. Why? Because if your life contradicts what you say, nobody's going to believe you anyway.

So first, you need to live out a godly life. But then you have to tell others about Christ—otherwise how will they know about Him, or your connection to Him? It would be like bringing a friend into a room and not introducing him to your other friends.

A Special Note on Witnessing to Family Members

Telling family members about Christ presents difficult challenges—but they can be overcome with time and patience.

Believe it or not, it's easier to talk about Jesus Christ with strangers than it is to tell your family members about Him. Why is this? Because the better you know someone in your family, the better they know you—and all of your inconsistencies, contradictions, weaknesses, and failures. Sometimes they use your faults as a reason not to become a Christian.

That's why, if you have an unsaved father, mother, husband, or wife, it's important to develop a long-term, consistent example of love and honesty toward them. You need to let them see Jesus in your life. But that doesn't mean you try to be a superpious, superspiritual saint in front of them. Don't feel that if you ever fail at being a "good Christian," you've failed God and they may go to hell because of you. Everyone makes his or her own choice. Rather, live a balanced, loving life in front of them, to the best of your human ability. Then, when you fail, talk to them. Tell them that you've failed, but God has forgiven you. Then ask for their forgiveness.

Although 1 Peter 3:1-2 was originally directed at women whose husbands were not Christians, the apostle Peter's words work for any situation with non-Christians: "Your godly lives will speak to them better than any words. They will be won over by watching your pure, godly behavior." Letting others know the truth and loving them in a long-term, patient relationship is the best introduction to Christ you could possibly give.

CHAPTER NINE

Choosing the Right Church

To continue growing in your Christian life, it's very important that you become part of a good church. Why is this important? Because a good church will provide you with instruction, accountability, encouragement, fellowship with other believers, and a worship experience.

And not only do you need a church, but a church needs you. That's because God has gifted each of us with abilities to share with others. A good church will expect you to use your gifts and abilities to benefit the group, and the exercise of your gifts will cause you to grow spiritually. What a terrific partnership!

FIVE CHARACTERISTICS OF A GODLY CHURCH

The key to a positive church experience is choosing the right church. Whether you're already part of a church or have never been inside one, it's important to make sure the church you choose to connect with has *all* five of the following characteristics.

#1: It's a place where Jesus Christ is communicated.

A good church will present Jesus Christ as the one and only answer to sin and this sinful world and will give men and women the opportunity to know Him. It's a place where evangelism is practiced, witnessing is encouraged, and where there are meetings where people can come to know Jesus Christ, even in the service. That does not mean there has to be a public invitation at every service, but that there are frequent opportunities to meet Christ, become born again, and changed spiritually.

#2: It has a positive, hopeful atmosphere.

Of all people in this world, Christians should be the most hopeful. Why? Because we have the sole answer and the joy that comes from knowing God's Son personally. This Bible passage about the early church illustrates the kind of positive community such a group can share:

All the believers met together constantly and shared everything they had. They sold their possessions and shared the proceeds with those in need. They worshiped together at the Temple each day, met in homes for the Lord's Supper, and shared their meals with great joy and generosity—all the while praising God and enjoying the goodwill of all the people. And

each day the Lord added to their group
those who were being saved. ACTS 2:44-47

Church should be a joyful experience,
embracing lives led in hope and goodwill. If
such is not the atmosphere, you're not in a
godly church.

#3: It's not perfect.

Are you surprised by this one? Well, if you're
trying to find the perfect church, you won't
find it. The old saying is that if there was a
perfect church, don't join it or you'll ruin it!
All churches have problems—even the early
church (see Acts 6:1-7 for an example)—
because human beings are sinful. But you can
accept that reality and then still work to find
the best church possible.

#4: It emphasizes the Bible and Bible study.

You need a church where the Bible is believed
and preached as the Word of God, where the
message of Jesus Christ is communicated. In
the early church, the believers "devoted themselves to the apostles' teaching" (Acts 2:42).
The apostles' teaching on the life of Christ
(that later became parts of the New Testament) was pertinent and crucial to the
growth of the early church. You, too, need
regular Bible study and teaching in order to
understand God's commands and truth.

That's why you shouldn't become
involved (or stay involved) in a congregation

that doesn't believe all of the Bible. For instance, if a church is weak on their stand against homosexuality and abortion, if they don't believe in the Bible as the inerrant, inspired Word of God, it would be best for you to leave and continue your spiritual growth in a church that is solidly grounded in Scripture.

#5: It encourages everyone to get involved. When you find a good church, get involved. Everybody—including you—has a vital role to play in the body of Christ. As the apostle Paul writes:

> *There are different kinds of spiritual gifts, but it is the same Holy Spirit who is the source of them all. There are different kinds of service in the church, but it is the same Lord we are serving. There are different ways God works in our lives, but it is the same God who does the work through all of us. A spiritual gift is given to each of us as a means of helping the entire church.* 1 CORINTHIANS 12:4-7

You may hear of Christians talking about "the body of Christ." By "the body," they mean the believers who are Christ's followers. In 1 Corinthians, Paul explains:

> *The human body has many parts, but the many parts make up only one body. So it is with the body of Christ. . . .*

*If one part suffers, all the parts suffer
with it, and if one part is honored, all the
parts are glad.*

*Now all of you together are Christ's
body, and each one of you is a separate
and necessary part of it.*   12:12, 26-27

Just as your body needs eyes, ears, feet, and
every single cell to function effectively, every
member of Christ's body brings a different
ability that helps the body of Christ work
more effectively.

That means each of us has something
special, something unique to contribute to the
church. And as we contribute, not only will
the church grow, but you'll further deepen
your own spiritual root system!

CHAPTER TEN

So What's Next?

Now that you've been introduced to Jesus Christ and to the steps you need to take to help you develop a spiritual root system, you have a choice to make. Will you choose to spend time growing spiritually—even when your schedule grows busy? Will you take time out to read your Bible, to listen to God's wisdom through His Holy Spirit's daily presence in your life, to communicate through prayer with your Father and Creator? Will you pursue discovering your spiritual gifts and then put them into use in a local church? Will you risk sharing your faith with others—even when it feels uncomfortable?

If so, the benefits will be incredible. Here are just a few of the verses (there are hundreds more in the Bible) that tell you what's ahead for you if you seek God with all your heart, soul, and mind:

> *Stay on the path that the Lord your God has commanded you to follow. Then you will live long and prosperous lives.*
>
> DEUTERONOMY 5:33

God is our refuge and strength, always ready to help in times of trouble.

PSALM 46:1

I wait quietly before God, for my hope is in him. He alone is my rock and my salvation, my fortress where I will not be shaken. PSALM 62:5-6

The Lord is wonderfully good to those who wait for him and seek him.

LAMENTATIONS 3:25

The Sovereign Lord is my strength! He will make me as surefooted as a deer and bring me safely over the mountains.

HABAKKUK 3:19

I assure you, those who listen to my message and believe in God who sent me have eternal life. JOHN 5:24

Don't be troubled. You trust God, now trust in me. There are many rooms in my Father's home, and I am going to prepare a place for you. JOHN 14:1-2

Now glory be to God! By his mighty power at work within us, he is able to accomplish infinitely more than we would ever dare to ask or hope.

EPHESIANS 3:20

And this same God who takes care of me will supply all your needs from his glori-

ous riches, which have been given to us in Christ Jesus. PHILIPPIANS 4:19

Let us come boldly to the throne of our gracious God. There we will receive his mercy, and we will find grace to help us when we need it. HEBREWS 4:16

And God, in his mighty power, will protect you until you receive this salvation, because you are trusting him. . . . So be truly glad! There is wonderful joy ahead, even though it is necessary for you to endure many trials for a while.
These trials are only to test your faith, to show that it is strong and pure. It is being tested as fire tests and purifies gold—and your faith is far more precious to God than mere gold. So if your faith remains strong after being tried by fiery trials, it will bring you much praise and glory and honor on the day when Jesus Christ is revealed to the whole world.
1 PETER 1:5-7

What wonderful earthly *and* heavenly rewards you have when you choose to follow Christ! You have the forgiveness of sins, daily help for life on this earth, and an eternal home with God. And that's not all—as you search the Scriptures, you'll discover a treasure chest of many more benefits. You might want to memorize some of them, write them on cards to carry with you, or even do a study of all the promises in the Bible.

As you continue on your spiritual journey to become more Christlike, life won't always be easy. But as you "Love the Lord your God with all your heart, all your soul, and all your strength" and you "commit yourselves wholeheartedly to these commands [He is] giving you today," (Deuteronomy 6:5-6), you are given many benefits and blessings in return. And at the very end of the Bible you're given a glorious promise that puts today's troubled world in perspective: "Yes, I am coming soon!" (Revelation 22:20). If you're a Christian, you can respond, with the apostle John, who wrote this last book of the Bible, "Amen! Come, Lord Jesus!"

CHAPTER ELEVEN

Helps for Christian Growth

RECOMMENDED READING

GUIDES TO WITNESSING

Roman Road. The plan of salvation through a selection of verses in Romans.

The Four Spiritual Laws (Campus Crusade). A simple explanation of the gospel that has been used by Campus Crusade for decades.

Becoming a Contagious Christian by Bill Hybels (Zondervan Publishing House). A motivating book on learning to share Christianity with others.

Explaining Your Faith by Alister McGrath (Baker Books). Brief, intelligible responses answer the questions most likely to be asked about your faith.

Out of the Salt Shaker and into the World by Rebecca Pippert (InterVarsity Press). An upbeat, encouraging guide to sharing your faith.

Learning about Christianity

Answers by Josh McDowell and Don Stewart (Tyndale House Publishers). The authors tackle sixty-five of the most-asked questions on the Bible, God, Jesus Christ, miracles, other religions, and creation in a question-and-answer format.

Christianity: Hoax or History? by Josh McDowell (Tyndale House Publishers). A popular speaker and author answers key objections to the Christian faith today. McDowell's evidence will challenge seeker and believer alike. A helpful, concise reference tool.

Christianity: The Faith That Makes Sense by Dennis McCallum (Tyndale House Publishers). This apologetic work presents a clear, rational defense for Christianity to those unfamiliar with the Bible and challenges readers to meet Christ personally.

Evidence That Demands a Verdict by Josh McDowell (Thomas Nelson). A great point-by-point handbook on evidence for numerous questions that seekers may have about evolution and creation, who Jesus is, whether his resurrection really happened, etc.

Does It Matter What I Believe? by Millard J. Erickson (Baker Books). The basics of

Christian faith presented thoughtfully and warmly by a well-known Christian scholar. Includes questions for group study.

If There's a God, Why Are There Atheists? by R. C. Sproul (Tyndale House Publishers). This is a book for Christians who have doubts or who want to know how to respond intelligently to nonbelievers and skeptics.

Mere Christianity by C. S. Lewis (HarperSanFrancisco). An apologetic work that builds a case for Christianity from reason and experience alone.

More Than a Carpenter by Josh McDowell (Tyndale House Publishers). A hard-hitting book for people who are skeptical about Jesus' deity, his resurrection, and his claim on their lives.

The Positive Power of Jesus Christ by Norman Vincent Peale (Tyndale House Publishers). Peale's strong, clear, and living witness to his faith in Jesus. He also relates true stories about others who have experienced the positive power of Jesus Christ.

Reasons by Josh McDowell and Don Stewart (Tyndale House Publishers). In a convenient question-and-answer format, the authors address many of the commonly asked questions on the Bible and evolution.

Skeptics Who Demanded a Verdict by Josh McDowell (Tyndale House Publishers). A booklet containing the stories of three one-time skeptics who came to believe in Christ: C. S. Lewis, Charles Colson, and Josh McDowell.

PRAYER

Adventures in Prayer by Catherine Marshall (Chosen Books). Refreshing insights about how surprisingly down-to-earth God wants our prayers to be.

God's Transmitters by Hannah Hurnard (Tyndale House Publishers). As God's children we are called to be transmitters of his love through prayer. By practicing the principles of faith and love, prayer becomes a joyful privilege in serving God.

Handle with Prayer by Charles Stanley (Chariot Victor). This book is a practical guide about praying.

How to Listen to God by Charles Stanley (Thomas Nelson). Another practical book on how to really develop an exciting, powerful, dynamic walk with God.

How to Pray for Your Family and Friends by Quin Sherrer (Vine Books). Releasing God's power in the lives of your spouse, parents, siblings, neighbors, and even your enemies.

Prayer: Finding the Heart's True Home by Richard J. Foster (Harper Collins). Discover a more intimate relationship with God through prayer.

What Happens When Women Pray by Evelyn Christenson (Chariot Victor). A practical book about how to develop an exciting prayer life. Written in an easy-to-read manner.

When God Says No by Leith Anderson (Bethany House). Discovering the God of hope behind the answer we'd rather not hear.

CONTINUED GROWTH

Celebration of Discipline by Richard J. Foster (Harper Collins). The path to spiritual growth through spiritual disciplines.

Essential Truths of the Christian Faith by R. C. Sproul (Tyndale House Publishers). The author offers a basic understanding of the Christian faith that is interesting and easy to read. More than 100 doctrines are categorized under major headings for easy reference.

Experiencing God by Henry T. Blackaby and Claude V. King (Broadman and Holman

Publishers). How to live the full adventure of knowing and doing the will of God.

Knowing God by J. I. Packer (InterVarsity Press). The author describes various aspects of God's character, such as His majesty, His wisdom, His grace, etc., and shows how each should affect believers.

Newborn by Jack Hayford (Tyndale House Publishers). Hayford discusses the newborn believer's relationship to God, how the Bible can help the believer, types of baptisms, and the importance of spending time with other believers.

Now, That's a Good Question! by R. C. Sproul (Tyndale House Publishers). Theologian Sproul answers more than 300 spiritual questions asked by ordinary people interested in the Christian faith and lifestyle.

Practical Christianity (Tyndale House Publishers). This book contains more than 200 original articles from leaders, authors, and speakers on the whys and how-tos of Christian growth and the process of living the Christian life today.

Bible Study

What the Bible Is All About by Henrietta C. Mears (Tyndale House Publishers).

Featuring *The Living Bible* text, this best-selling book offers a clear, concise overview of the Scriptures, one book at a time. An invaluable resource.

THE ONE YEAR NEW TESTAMENT READING PLAN

JANUARY 1 Matthew 1:1–2:12

JANUARY 2 Matthew 2:13–3:6

JANUARY 3 Matthew 3:7–4:11

JANUARY 4 Matthew 4:12-25

JANUARY 5 Matthew 5:1-26

JANUARY 6 Matthew 5:27-48

JANUARY 7 Matthew 6:1-24

JANUARY 8 Matthew 6:25–7:14

JANUARY 9 Matthew 7:15-29

JANUARY 10 Matthew 8:1-17

JANUARY 11 Matthew 8:18-34

JANUARY 12 Matthew 9:1-17

JANUARY 13 Matthew 9:18-38

JANUARY 14 Matthew 10:1-23

JANUARY 15 Matthew 10:24–11:6

JANUARY 16 Matthew 11:7-30

JANUARY 17 Matthew 12:1-21

JANUARY 18 Matthew 12:22-45

JANUARY 19 Matthew 12:46–13:23

JANUARY 20 Matthew 13:24-46

JANUARY 21 Matthew 13:47–14:12

JANUARY 22 Matthew 14:13-36

JANUARY 23 Matthew 15:1-28

JANUARY 24 Matthew 15:29–16:12

JANUARY 25 Matthew 16:13–17:9

JANUARY 26 Matthew 17:10-27

JANUARY 27 Matthew 18:1-22

JANUARY 28 Matthew 18:23–19:12

JANUARY 29 Matthew 19:13-30

JANUARY 30 Matthew 20:1-28

JANUARY 31 Matthew 20:29–21:22

FEBRUARY 1 Matthew 21:23-46

FEBRUARY 2 Matthew 22:1-33

FEBRUARY 3 Matthew 22:34–23:12

FEBRUARY 4 Matthew 23:13-39

FEBRUARY 5 Matthew 24:1-28

FEBRUARY 6 Matthew 24:29-51

FEBRUARY 7 Matthew 25:1-30

FEBRUARY 8 Matthew 25:31–26:13

February 9 Matthew 26:14-46

February 10 Matthew 26:47-68

February 11 Matthew 26:69–27:14

February 12 Matthew 27:15-31

February 13 Matthew 27:32-66

February 14 Matthew 28:1-20

February 15 Mark 1:1-28

February 16 Mark 1:29–2:12

February 17 Mark 2:13–3:6

February 18 Mark 3:7-30

February 19 Mark 3:31–4:25

February 20 Mark 4:26–5:20

February 21 Mark 5:21-43

February 22 Mark 6:1-29

February 23 Mark 6:30-56

February 24 Mark 7:1-23

February 25 Mark 7:24–8:10

February 26 Mark 8:11-38

February 27 Mark 9:1-29

February 28 Mark 9:30–10:12

March 1 Mark 10:13-31

March 2 Mark 10:32-52

MARCH 3 Mark 11:1-25

MARCH 4 Mark 11:27–12:17

MARCH 5 Mark 12:18-37

MARCH 6 Mark 12:38–13:13

MARCH 7 Mark 13:14-37

MARCH 8 Mark 14:1-21

MARCH 9 Mark 14:22-52

MARCH 10 Mark 14:53-72

MARCH 11 Mark 15:1-47

MARCH 12 Mark 16:1-20

MARCH 13 Luke 1:1-25

MARCH 14 Luke 1:26-56

MARCH 15 Luke 1:57-80

MARCH16 Luke 2:1-35

MARCH 17 Luke 2:36-52

MARCH 18 Luke 3:1-22

MARCH 19 Luke 3:23-38

MARCH 20 Luke 4:1-30

MARCH 21 Luke 4:31–5:11

MARCH 22 Luke 5:12-28

MARCH 23 Luke 5:29–6:11

MARCH 24 Luke 6:12-38

MARCH 25 Luke 6:39–7:10

MARCH 26 Luke 7:11-35

MARCH 27 Luke 7:36–8:3

MARCH 28 Luke 8:4-21

MARCH 29 Luke 8:22-39

MARCH 30 Luke 8:40–9:6

MARCH 31 Luke 9:7-27

APRIL 1 Luke 9:28-50

APRIL 2 Luke 9:51–10:12

APRIL 3 Luke 10:13-37

APRIL 4 Luke 10:38–11:13

APRIL 5 Luke 11:14-36

APRIL 6 Luke 11:37–12:7

APRIL 7 Luke 12:8-34

APRIL 8 Luke 12:35-59

APRIL 9 Luke 13:1-21

APRIL 10 Luke 13:22–14:6

APRIL 11 Luke 14:7-35

APRIL 12 Luke 15:1-32

APRIL 13 Luke 16:1-18

APRIL 14 Luke 16:19–17:10

APRIL 15 Luke 17:11-37

APRIL 16 Luke 18:1-17

APRIL 17 Luke 18:18-43

APRIL 18 Luke 19:1-27

APRIL 19 Luke 19:28-48

APRIL 20 Luke 20:1-26

APRIL 21 Luke 20:27-47

APRIL 22 Luke 21:1-28

APRIL 23 Luke 21:29–22:13

APRIL 24 Luke 22:14-34

APRIL 25 Luke 22:35-53

APRIL 26 Luke 22:54–23:12

APRIL 27 Luke 23:13-43

APRIL 28 Luke 23:44–24:12

APRIL 29 Luke 24:13-53

APRIL 30 John 1:1-28

MAY 1 John 1:29-51

MAY 2 John 2:1-25

MAY 3 John 3:1-21

MAY 4 John 3:22–4:3

MAY 5 John 4:4-42

MAY 6 John 4:43-54

MAY 7 John 5:1-23

MAY 8 John 5:24-47

MAY 9 John 6:1-21

MAY 10 John 6:22-42

MAY 11 John 6:43-71

MAY 12 John 7:1-30

MAY 13 John 7:31-53

MAY 14 John 8:1-20

MAY 15 John 8:21-30

MAY 16 John 8:31-59

MAY 17 John 9:1-41

MAY 18 John 10:1-21

MAY 19 John 10:22-42

MAY 20 John 11:1-54

MAY 21 John 11:55–12:19

MAY 22 John 12:20-50

MAY 23 John 13:1-30

MAY 24 John 13:31–14:14

MAY 25 John 14:15-31

MAY 26 John 15:1-27

MAY 27 John 16:1-33

MAY 28 John 17:1-26

MAY 29 John 18:1-24

MAY 30 John 18:25–19:22

MAY 31 John 19:23-42

JUNE 1 John 20:1-31

JUNE 2 John 21:1-25

JUNE 3 Acts 1:1-26

JUNE 4 Acts 2:1-47

JUNE 5 Acts 3:1-26

JUNE 6 Acts 4:1-37

JUNE 7 Acts 5:1-42

JUNE 8 Acts 6:1-15

JUNE 9 Acts 7:1-29

JUNE 10 Acts 7:30-50

JUNE 11 Acts 7:51–8:13

JUNE 12 Acts 8:14-40

JUNE 13 Acts 9:1-25

JUNE 14 Acts 9:26-43

JUNE 15 Acts 10:1-23

JUNE 16 Acts 10:24-48

JUNE 17 Acts 11:1-30

JUNE 18 Acts 12:1-23

JUNE 19 Acts 12:24–13:15

JUNE 20 Acts 13:16-41

June 21 Acts 13:42–14:7

June 22 Acts 14:8-28

June 23 Acts 15:1-35

June 24 Acts 15:36–16:15

June 25 Acts 16:16-40

June 26 Acts 17:1-34

June 27 Acts 18:1-22

June 28 Acts 18:23–19:12

June 29 Acts 19:13-41

June 30 Acts 20:1-38

July 1 Acts 21:1-17

July 2 Acts 21:18-36

July 3 Acts 21:37–22:16

July 4 Acts 22:17–23:10

July 5 Acts 23:11-35

July 6 Acts 24:1-27

July 7 Acts 25:1-27

July 8 Acts 26:1-32

July 9 Acts 27:1-20

July 10 Acts 27:21-44

July 11 Acts 28:1-31

July 12 Romans 1:1-17

JULY 13 Romans 1:18-32

JULY 14 Romans 2:1-24

JULY 15 Romans 2:25–3:8

JULY 16 Romans 3:9-31

JULY 17 Romans 4:1-12

JULY 18 Romans 4:13–5:5

JULY 19 Romans 5:6-21

JULY 20 Romans 6:1-23

JULY 21 Romans 7:1-13

JULY 22 Romans 7:14–8:8

JULY 23 Romans 8:9-25

JULY 24 Romans 8:26-39

JULY 25 Romans 9:1-24

JULY 26 Romans 9:25–10:13

JULY 27 Romans 10:14–11:12

JULY 28 Romans 11:13-36

JULY 29 Romans 12:1-21

JULY 30 Romans 13:1-14

JULY 31 Romans 14:1-23

AUGUST 1 Romans 15:1-22

AUGUST 2 Romans 15:23–16:9

AUGUST 3 Romans 16:10-27

August 4   1 Corinthians 1:1-17

August 5   1 Corinthians 1:18–2:5

August 6   1 Corinthians 2:6–3:4

August 7   1 Corinthians 3:5-23

August 8   1 Corinthians 4:1-21

August 9   1 Corinthians 5:1-13

August 10   1 Corinthians 6:1-20

August 11   1 Corinthians 7:1-24

August 12   1 Corinthians 7:25-40

August 13   1 Corinthians 8:1-13

August 14   1 Corinthians 9:1-18

August 15   1 Corinthians 9:19–10:13

August 16   1 Corinthians 10:14-33

August 17   1 Corinthians 11:1-16

August 18   1 Corinthians 11:17-34

August 19   1 Corinthians 12:1-26

August 20   1 Corinthians 12:27–13:13

August 21   1 Corinthians 14:1-17

August 22   1 Corinthians 14:18-40

August 23   1 Corinthians 15:1-28

August 24   1 Corinthians 15:29-58

August 25   1 Corinthians 16:1-24

AUGUST 26 2 Corinthians 1:1-11

AUGUST 27 2 Corinthians 1:12–2:11

AUGUST 28 2 Corinthians 2:12-17

AUGUST 29 2 Corinthians 3:1-18

AUGUST 30 2 Corinthians 4:1-12

AUGUST 31 2 Corinthians 4:13–5:10

SEPTEMBER 1 2 Corinthians 5:11-21

SEPTEMBER 2 2 Corinthians 6:1-13

SEPTEMBER 3 2 Corinthians 6:14–7:7

SEPTEMBER 4 2 Corinthians 7:8-16

SEPTEMBER 5 2 Corinthians 8:1-15

SEPTEMBER 6 2 Corinthians 8:16-24

SEPTEMBER 7 2 Corinthians 9:1-15

SEPTEMBER 8 2 Corinthians 10:1-18

SEPTEMBER 9 2 Corinthians 11:1-15

SEPTEMBER 10 2 Corinthians 11:16-33

SEPTEMBER 11 2 Corinthians 12:1-10

SEPTEMBER 12 2 Corinthians 12:11-21

SEPTEMBER 13 2 Corinthians 13:1-13

SEPTEMBER 14 Galatians 1:1-24

SEPTEMBER 15 Galatians 2:1-16

SEPTEMBER 16 Galatians 2:17–3:9

SEPTEMBER 17 Galatians 3:10-22

SEPTEMBER 18 Galatians 3:23–4:31

SEPTEMBER 19 Galatians 5:1-12

SEPTEMBER 20 Galatians 5:13-26

SEPTEMBER 21 Galatians 6:1-18

SEPTEMBER 22 Ephesians 1:1-23

SEPTEMBER 23 Ephesians 2:1-22

SEPTEMBER 24 Ephesians 3:1-21

SEPTEMBER 25 Ephesians 4:1-16

SEPTEMBER 26 Ephesians 4:17-32

SEPTEMBER 27 Ephesians 5:1-33

SEPTEMBER 28 Ephesians 6:1-24

SEPTEMBER 29 Philippians 1:1-26

SEPTEMBER 30 Philippians 1:27–2:18

OCTOBER 1 Philippians 2:19–3:3

OCTOBER 2 Philippians 3:4-21

OCTOBER 3 Philippians 4:1-23

OCTOBER 4 Colossians 1:1-17

OCTOBER 5 Colossians 1:18–2:7

OCTOBER 6 Colossians 2:8-23

OCTOBER 7 Colossians 3:1-17

OCTOBER 8 Colossians 3:18–4:18

OCTOBER 9 1 Thessalonians 1:1–2:8

OCTOBER 10 1 Thessalonians 2:9–3:13

OCTOBER 11 1 Thessalonians 4:1–5:3

OCTOBER 12 1 Thessalonians 5:4-28

OCTOBER 13 2 Thessalonians 1:1-12

OCTOBER 14 2 Thessalonians 2:1-17

OCTOBER 15 2 Thessalonians 3:1-18

OCTOBER 16 1 Timothy 1:1-20

OCTOBER 17 1 Timothy 2:1-15

OCTOBER 18 1 Timothy 3:1-16

OCTOBER 19 1 Timothy 4:1-16

OCTOBER 20 1 Timothy 5:1-25

OCTOBER 21 1 Timothy 6:1-21

OCTOBER 22 2 Timothy 1:1-18

OCTOBER 23 2 Timothy 2:1-21

OCTOBER 24 2 Timothy 2:22–3:17

OCTOBER 25 2 Timothy 4:1-22

OCTOBER 26 Titus 1:1-16

OCTOBER 27 Titus 2:1-15

OCTOBER 28 Titus 3:1-15

OCTOBER 29 Philemon 1:1-25

OCTOBER 30 Hebrews 1:1-14

OCTOBER 31 Hebrews 2:1-18

NOVEMBER 1 Hebrews 3:1-19

NOVEMBER 2 Hebrews 4:1-16

NOVEMBER 3 Hebrews 5:1-14

NOVEMBER 4 Hebrews 6:1-20

NOVEMBER 5 Hebrews 7:1-17

NOVEMBER 6 Hebrews 7:18-28

NOVEMBER 7 Hebrews 8:1-13

NOVEMBER 8 Hebrews 9:1-10

NOVEMBER 9 Hebrews 9:11-28

NOVEMBER 10 Hebrews 10:1-17

NOVEMBER 11 Hebrews 10:18-39

NOVEMBER 12 Hebrews 11:1-16

NOVEMBER 13 Hebrews 11:17-31

NOVEMBER 14 Hebrews 11:32–12:13

NOVEMBER 15 Hebrews 12:14-29

NOVEMBER 16 Hebrews 13:1-25

NOVEMBER 17 James 1:1-18

NOVEMBER 18 James 1:19–2:17

NOVEMBER 19 James 2:18–3:18

NOVEMBER 20 James 4:1-17

NOVEMBER 21 James 5:1-20

NOVEMBER 22 1 Peter 1:1-12

NOVEMBER 23 1 Peter 1:13–2:10

NOVEMBER 24 1 Peter 2:11–3:7

NOVEMBER 25 1 Peter 3:8–4:6

NOVEMBER 26 1 Peter 4:7–5:14

NOVEMBER 27 2 Peter 1:1-21

NOVEMBER 28 2 Peter 2:1-22

NOVEMBER 29 2 Peter 3:1-18

NOVEMBER 30 1 John 1:1-10

DECEMBER 1 1 John 2:1-17

DECEMBER 2 1 John 2:18–3:6

DECEMBER 3 1 John 3:7-24

DECEMBER 4 1 John 4:1-21

DECEMBER 5 1 John 5:1-21

DECEMBER 6 2 John 1:1-13

DECEMBER 7 3 John 1:1-15

DECEMBER 8 Jude 1:1-25

DECEMBER 9 Revelation 1:1-20

DECEMBER 10 Revelation 2:1-17

DECEMBER 11 Revelation 2:18–3:6

DECEMBER 12 Revelation 3:7-22

DECEMBER 13 Revelation 4:1-11

December 14 Revelation 5:1-14

December 15 Revelation 6:1-17

December 16 Revelation 7:1-17

December 17 Revelation 8:1-13

December 18 Revelation 9:1-21

December 19 Revelation 10:1-11

December 20 Revelation 11:1-19

December 21 Revelation 12:1-17

December 22 Revelation 12:18–3:18

December 23 Revelation 14:1-20

December 24 Revelation 15:1-8

December 25 Revelation 16:1-21

December 26 Revelation 17:1-18

December 27 Revelation 18:1-24

December 28 Revelation 19:1-21

December 29 Revelation 20:1-15

December 30 Revelation 21:1-27

December 31 Revelation 22:1-21

Favorite Bible Passage Index

Great Topics

CREATION Genesis 1:1–2:7
PASSOVER Exodus 12
COMMANDMENTS Exodus 20
COMMITMENT Deuteronomy 6
GOD'S LOVE Psalm 23
REPENTANCE Psalm 51
GOD'S LAWS Psalm 119
GOD'S KNOWLEDGE Psalm 139
WISDOM Proverbs 1
A GODLY WOMAN Proverbs 31
TIMING Ecclesiastes 3
ISAIAH'S VISION Isaiah 6
SIGN OF IMMANUEL Isaiah 7
THE SUFFERING SERVANT Isaiah 52:13–53:12
GOD'S POWER Jeremiah 18
ISRAEL'S WATCHMAN Ezekiel 33
HEALING OF SINS Hosea 14
SERMON ON THE MOUNT Matthew 5–7
GREATEST COMMANDMENT Mark 12:28-34
PARABLES OF THE LOST Luke 15
THE ETERNAL WORD John 1
THE HOLY SPIRIT John 14–16
PETER'S SERMON Acts 2
SALVATION Romans 3
LOVE 1 Corinthians 13
DEPENDENCE 2 Corinthians 12
SPIRITUAL ARMOR Ephesians 6:10-20
CHRIST'S HUMILITY Philippians 2
RIGHTEOUS LIVING Colossians 3

Leadership 1 Timothy 3
Faith Hebrews 11
Temptation James 1
Suffering 1 Peter 4
Fellowship 1 John 1
Heaven Revelation 21–22

Great Stories

Cain and Abel Genesis 4:1-16
The Flood Genesis 6:1–9:17
The Tower of Babel Genesis 11:1-9
Abraham's Call Genesis 12:1-9
Abraham's Obedience Genesis 22:1-19
Joseph as a Slave Genesis 37:18-36
Moses Is Born Exodus 2:1-10
The Burning Bush Exodus 3:1-22
The Ten Plagues Exodus 7:14–12:30
The Exodus Exodus 12:31-51
The Red Sea Exodus 14:21-31
The Gold Calf Exodus 32:1-29
The Twelve Scouts Numbers 13:1-33
The Bronze Snake Numbers 21:4-9
Jericho Falls Joshua 6:1-27
Gideon as Judge Judges 6:1–7:25
Samson as Judge Judges 13:1–16:31
God Provides for Ruth Ruth 1:1–4:22
Samuel Is Born 1 Samuel 1:1-28
David Kills Goliath 1 Samuel 17:1-51
David and Jonathan 1 Samuel 18:1-4;
    20:1-42

DAVID AND BATHSHEBA 2 Samuel 11:1-27
SOLOMON JUDGES WISELY 1 Kings 3:16-28
ELIJAH'S CHALLENGE 1 Kings 18:1-40
GOD SPEAKS TO ELIJAH 1 Kings 19:1-18
ELISHA HEALS NAAMAN 2 Kings 5:1-19
DAVID'S MIGHTY MEN 1 Chronicles 11:10-25
ESTHER SAVES THE JEWS Esther 1:1–10:3
JOB TESTED Job 1:1-22
EZEKIEL'S VISION Ezekiel 37:1-14
THE FIERY FURNACE Daniel 3:1-30
THE LIONS' DEN Daniel 6:1-28
JONAH AND THE FISH Jonah 1:1–2:10
JESUS IS BORN Matthew 1:18-25; Luke 2:1-20
WISE MEN VISIT JESUS Matthew 2:1-12
JESUS IS TEMPTED Matthew 4:1-11;
    Mark 1:12-13; Luke 4:1-13
JESUS WALKS ON WATER Matthew 14:22-33;
    Mark 6:45-52; John 6:16-21
THE GOOD SAMARITAN Luke 10:25-37
THE LOST SON Luke 15:11-32
JESUS FEEDS FIVE THOUSAND Matthew 14:13-
    21; Mark 6:30-44; Luke 9:10-17;
    John 6:1-15
JESUS RAISES LAZARUS John 11:1-44
JESUS AND ZACCHAEUS Luke 19:1-10
THE TRIUMPHAL ENTRY Matthew 21:1-11;
    Luke 19:28-40; John 12:12-19
THE LAST SUPPER Matthew 26:17-30; Mark
    14:12-26; Luke 22:7-30; John 13:1-30
JESUS' CRUCIFIXION Matthew 27:32-56;
    Mark 15:21-41; Luke 23:26-49;
    John 19:16b-37

RON BALL

JESUS' RESURRECTION Matthew 28:1-15;
    Mark 16:1-14; Luke 24:1-12; John 20:1-10
JESUS' ASCENSION Luke 24:50-53; Acts 1:6-11
THE HOLY SPIRIT Acts 2:1-13
ANANIAS AND SAPPHIRA Acts 5:1-11
SAUL ENCOUNTERS JESUS Acts 9:1-19
PAUL IS SHIPWRECKED Acts 27:1–28:10

TYNDALE BIBLE VERSE FINDER

Abortion

MARK 9:36-37 Welcoming children is welcoming Christ.

LUKE 18:15-17 Jesus welcomed children.

Abuse

MATTHEW 26:67-68 Jesus was abused.

EPHESIANS 5:21–6:4 Abuse has no place in family relationships.

Accountability

MATTHEW 12:36 We are accountable for every word that we speak.

MATTHEW 18:15 Confronting others with their sins should be done in private.

LUKE 17:3 We should hold each other accountable.

JOHN 3:18 We are accountable for what we believe.

ROMANS 14:11-12 God holds Christians accountable.

1 CORINTHIANS 3:8 God will reward Christians for their good deeds.

2 CORINTHIANS 5:10 God will examine our actions.

Accusations

MATTHEW 26:59-60 Jesus was falsely accused.

COLOSSIANS 1:22 Christians' sins are forgiven.

1 TIMOTHY 5:19 Accusations against church leaders must come from more than one person.

REVELATION 12:10 Satan is known as the Accuser.

Adolescence

1 TIMOTHY 4:12 Young people should be an example to others.

2 TIMOTHY 2:22 Young people should run from their youthful lust.

Adoption, spiritual

MATTHEW 6:9 Christians can address God as our Father.

JOHN 1:12 Christians are God's children.

ROMANS 8:14-17 God's Spirit leads his children.

2 CORINTHIANS 6:17-18 Christians should be separate from the world.

GALATIANS 3:28 All of God's children are equally accepted by him.

GALATIANS 4:4-7 God's children will receive a spiritual inheritance.

EPHESIANS 1:4-5 God chose us to be his children.

HEBREWS 2:11 Jesus is our spiritual brother.

Adultery

MATTHEW 5:27-28 God considers lust as sinful as adultery.

JOHN 8:1-11 God can forgive the adulterer.

Alcohol

ROMANS 13:13-14 Becoming drunk is sinful.

GALATIANS 5:19-21 God hates drunkenness.

TITUS 1:7 Church leaders especially should not be controlled by alcohol.

Anger

MATTHEW 5:21-26 Jesus teaches us to forgive.

MARK 3:5 Jesus became angry with those who were hard-hearted.

JOHN 2:13-17 Jesus grew angry at sin.

ROMANS 1:18-20 God shows anger toward those who reject the truth.

EPHESIANS 4:26-27 Anger can give Satan a place in your life.

COLOSSIANS 3:8 Christians should get rid of anger.

TITUS 1:7 Leaders in the church should not be quick-tempered.

JAMES 1:19 Be slow to become angry.

JAMES 3:5-6 Don't speak in anger.

(See also: Hatred, Revenge)

Appearance

MATTHEW 6:25-34 Do not worry about clothes.

MATTHEW 23:27 Appearances can be deceiving.

1 TIMOTHY 2:9-10 Christians should care more about their spiritual welfare than their physical appearance.

JAMES 2:2-4 Do not judge others by their appearance.

1 PETER 3:1-6 Inner beauty is more important than physical beauty.

(See also: Clothing)

Approval

JOSHUA 23:12-14 God doesn't approve of sin.

MATTHEW 10:32-33 Christ acknowledges those who acknowledge him.

JOHN 5:41 Jesus did not seek the approval of people.

John 8:54-59 God approves of telling the truth.

John 12:37-43 Many people prefer human approval over God's approval.

Arguments

Romans 14:1 Avoid arguing with a weak Christian.

Philippians 2:14 We should avoid arguments.

Titus 3:9 Foolish arguments about petty issues are useless.

Armor

Romans 13:12 Spiritual armor prepares us for life.

2 Corinthians 6:7 Righteousness is a spiritual weapon.

2 Corinthians 10:4 God's weapons conquer Satan's strongholds.

Ephesians 6:11-18 Put on the whole armor of God.

Assurance

Luke 18:18-30 False assurance is dangerous.

John 5:24 We can be assured of eternal life.

John 6:37-40 God will not refuse any who come to him.

John 10:27-28 Our place in God's family is secure.

Romans 5:1-5 Christians have peace with God.

ROMANS 8:35-39 Nothing can separate us from God's love.

ROMANS 11:29 Salvation cannot be canceled.

GALATIANS 6:1 Accountability should help others.

EPHESIANS 1:4-5 Our salvation was guaranteed before Creation.

EPHESIANS 3:12 Assurance comes from faith.

2 TIMOTHY 1:12 God will guard what has been entrusted to him.

Attitude

MATTHEW 5:3-12 Be happy and blessed by obeying God.

PHILIPPIANS 1:20-25 God gives Christians a new attitude.

PHILIPPIANS 2:5 We should imitate Jesus' attitude.

PHILIPPIANS 4:4 Christians should always rejoice.

PHILIPPIANS 4:6-7 Never be anxious.

Authority

MATTHEW 3:17 God gave Jesus authority.

MATTHEW 28:18 Jesus is the highest authority.

MARK 9:2-8 Jesus was under authority.

MARK 12:13-17 Jesus acknowledged the authority of both God and human government.

JOHN 19:11 God gave government its authority.

ACTS 4:7-12 Jesus is our authority.

ROMANS 13:1-7 Obey the authorities as long as they do not contradict God's commands.

1 CORINTHIANS 11:3, 11-12 We must all submit to authority in marriage.

EPHESIANS 6:1-3 Obey your parents.

1 THESSALONIANS 5:12-13 Honor church authorities.

2 TIMOTHY 3:16 The Bible is our authority.

HEBREWS 13:17 Church leaders hold authority over us.

(See also: Marriage, Parents, Respect)

Backsliding

LUKE 15:11-31 God waits for backsliders to return to him.

1 TIMOTHY 6:10 The love of money can cause backsliding.

JAMES 5:19-20 We should help backsliders return to God.

2 PETER 3:14-18 False teachers can lead Christians astray.

Baptism

MATTHEW 3:11 Baptism signifies repentance.

MATTHEW 28:19 All followers of Jesus should be baptized.

MARK 1:9 Jesus was baptized.

JOHN 1:32-33 Jesus baptizes with the Holy Spirit.

ACTS 2:38 Baptism is closely linked with a changed life.

ACTS 8:12-17 New Christians should be baptized.

ACTS 16:33-34 Entire families of the early church were baptized.

ROMANS 6:3-8 Baptism initiates us into Christ.

1 PETER 3:21 Salvation is identified with baptism.

Balanced life

LUKE 2:40, 52 Jesus became mature in every aspect of life.

ROMANS 6:12-14 Your body belongs to God.

ROMANS 12:1-2 Your body is an offering to God.

EPHESIANS 4:23-24 Our thoughts and actions should reflect that we are a new creation.

COLOSSIANS 3:9-17 Christians have new lives.

Belief

MARK 1:15 Changed lives should accompany right beliefs.

ROMANS 10:9 Right beliefs are important for salvation.

JAMES 2:21 Believing is more than acknowledging.

Bible

MATTHEW 4:3-4 The Bible can help us resist temptation.

ACTS 18:28 The Bible reveals truth.

ROMANS 1:2 The Bible is holy.

ROMANS 1:16-17 The Bible is good news.

1 CORINTHIANS 2:12-16 God's Holy Spirit helps us understand the Bible.

GALATIANS 3:10 The Bible is authoritative.

EPHESIANS 6:17 The Bible is a Christian's spiritual weapon.

2 TIMOTHY 3:16 The Bible is inspired by God.

HEBREWS 4:12 The Bible judges our life.

1 PETER 2:2 The Bible helps us grow spiritually.

2 PETER 1:16-21 Scripture is inspired by the Holy Spirit.

1 JOHN 2:12-17 The Bible has practical advice.

REVELATION 22:18-19 Don't change or add to the Bible.

(See also: Devotions, God's will)

Birth

LUKE 2:7 Jesus was born to Mary and Joseph.

JOHN 1:12-13 God's children are reborn spiritually.

JOHN 3:3 People must be reborn spiritually to enter heaven.

Blessing

MATTHEW 6:33 God blesses us when we seek to please him.

MARK 8:6 Jesus teaches by example to be thankful.

LUKE 6:28 Christians should bless their enemies.

EPHESIANS 1:3 God has blessed his children with salvation.

JAMES 1:25 God blesses us for obeying his word.

(See also: Thankfulness)

Blood

MATTHEW 26:28 Jesus' blood seals God's relationship with his people.

ROMANS 5:8-9 Jesus' blood allows us to have access to God.

EPHESIANS 1:5-7 Christians are redeemed by Jesus' blood.

HEBREWS 9:22 Blood is required for forgiveness.

Body of Christ

ROMANS 12:3-6 The body of Christ has been given many gifts.

1 CORINTHIANS 12:12-13 There are many parts, but one body.

1 CORINTHIANS 12:27 Christians make up the body of Christ.

EPHESIANS 3:6 Christians of different nationalities form one body.

EPHESIANS 4:3 There must be unity in the body of Christ.

EPHESIANS 4:11-12 Different members of the body help each other grow.

COLOSSIANS 1:18 Jesus is the head of the body.

Business

EPHESIANS 6:6-7 Work as though Jesus were your boss.

TITUS 2:9-10 Christians should do their best at their job.

Caring

LUKE 6:27 Care for your enemies.

LUKE 14:13-14 God's people should care for the needy.

JOHN 11:32-44 Jesus is our example.

ACTS 20:21-38 Caring causes others to care.

ROMANS 1:6-7 God cares for his children.

1 CORINTHIANS 9:19-23 How to show care when witnessing.

EPHESIANS 6:2 Treat parents with care.

COLOSSIANS 4:1 Treat co-workers with care.

1 TIMOTHY 5:1-4 Christians should care for one another.

JAMES 1:27 Christians should care for those who have no one to care for them.

(See also: Compassion, Serving others)

Character

MATTHEW 6:1-4 God recognizes our true character.

ROMANS 5:3-4 Learning to endure problems develops character, which helps us to confidently expect salvation.

Children

JOHN 1:12 Christians are children of God.

EPHESIANS 5:1 Children of God should imitate God.

EPHESIANS 6:4 Parents should nurture their children.

COLOSSIANS 3:20 Children must obey their parents.

Choices

MATTHEW 7:13-14 Choose the path that leads to life.

(See also: Decisions, Freedom)

Church

MATTHEW 16:18 Satan works against the church.

LUKE 4:16 Jesus worshiped God regularly in the synagogue.

JOHN 4:21-24 Right worship involves worshiping God in spirit and in truth.

ACTS 2:44 Members of the church should take care of each other.

ACTS 13:2 The church sends out missionaries.

ROMANS 12:4-21 The church is the body of Christ on earth.

1 CORINTHIANS 12:12-13 The church is like a body.

EPHESIANS 2:19-22 God's children form the church.

EPHESIANS 5:3-4 The church should not allow immoral behavior by its members.

COLOSSIANS 1:18 Christ is the head of the church.

Colossians 3:11 Many people groups form one universal church.

Titus 1:6-9 Church leaders are qualified to lead by their character.

Hebrews 10:25 Don't neglect church attendance.

1 John 3:1 The church is made up of God's children.

Revelation 19:7-8 The church is the bride of Christ.

(See also: Worship)

Clothing

Matthew 6:25-34 Don't worry about clothing.

Matthew 22:11-12 We must be clothed in righteousness to enter the Kingdom of God.

1 Peter 3:1-5 Clothing should be modest.

(See also: Appearance)

Comfort

Matthew 5:4 God promises to comfort those who mourn.

John 14:16 God's Holy Spirit is our Comforter.

John 16:33 Jesus has overcome the world and its troubles.

2 Corinthians 1:3-11 God comforts those who are hurting.

1 Thessalonians 4:18 Christians should comfort each other.

Revelation 21:3-4 One day all pain will end.

Commitment

Matthew 10:32-33 We must be committed to Christ.

Matthew 13:21 We must remain committed to Christ in tough times.

John 1:49 Nathanael showed decisive commitment to Jesus.

Acts 24:16 Paul was committed to maintaining a clear conscience before God.

Communication

James 1:19 Listen more than you talk.

(See also: Criticism, Gossip, Witnessing)

Compassion

Mark 3:3-5 Compassion means helping others less fortunate.

Matthew 14:14 Jesus is our example of compassion.

Luke 6:36 We are to be compassionate just as God is.

Luke 10:30-37 We should even have compassion on those we do not like.

Luke 15:3-7 God has great compassion for those who have wandered from him.

(See also: Caring, Serving others)

Complaining

MATTHEW 20:1-16 Envy can cause complaining.

PHILIPPIANS 2:14-16 Do everything without complaining.

JUDE 1:16 False teachers will be grumblers and complainers.

(See also: Contentment)

Compromise

MATTHEW 5:25 Sometimes we should compromise with others to be reconciled to them.

MARK 15:15 Compromise can keep us from doing what is right.

2 CORINTHIANS 6:14-18 Some compromise can weaken our faith.

Confession

LUKE 3:4-18 John called people to repent and turn from sin.

JAMES 5:16 We should confess our sins to other believers.

1 JOHN 1:8-10 God forgives our sins when we confess them.

(See also: Forgiveness, Repentance)

Conscience

ROMANS 9:1 The Holy Spirit works together with our conscience to speak to us.

ROMANS 14:23 Listen to your conscience.

1 TIMOTHY 1:18-19 Keep your conscience clear.

1 TIMOTHY 3:9 Church leaders must have clear consciences.

1 TIMOTHY 4:2 Many false teachers have deadened their consciences.

HEBREWS 9:14 Jesus' forgiveness clears our conscience.

1 PETER 3:16 Our best witness comes from a godly life and a clear conscience.

Consequences

MATTHEW 7:13-14 The path we choose in life will have definite consequences.

2 CORINTHIANS 5:10 Each of us will stand before God.

Contentment

MATTHEW 6:25-35 Be content with what you have.

JOHN 3:30 Contentment comes when you put Jesus first.

PHILIPPIANS 4:10-14 Be content in every situation.

(See also: Happiness)

Courage

JOHN 16:33 Jesus' victory over the world gives us courage.

ACTS 4:31 God's Holy Spirit fills us with courage to proclaim Christ.

1 CORINTHIANS 16:13 Christians should be courageous.

EPHESIANS 6:19-20 Pray for courage.

HEBREWS 4:16 Christians can pray to God with confidence.

Covenant

LUKE 22:20 Jesus established a new covenant in his blood.

2 CORINTHIANS 3:6 God's covenant brings life.

HEBREWS 8:6 The new covenant is superior to the old covenant.

HEBREWS 10:1 The old covenant foreshadowed the new covenant.

Creation

COLOSSIANS 1:16 Christ was involved in Creation.

REVELATION 4:11 God the Creator is worthy of worship.

REVELATION 21:1-4 God will make a new heaven and new earth.

Criticism

MATTHEW 7:1-6 Take care of your own problems before criticizing others.

LUKE 17:3-4 We should rebuke those who need correction.

GALATIANS 5:15 Harsh criticism can destroy rather than help.

1 PETER 3:16 Live above criticism.

(See also: Communication)

Cross

MATTHEW 27:31-35 Jesus was nailed to a cross.

MARK 8:34-38 Following Christ requires that we shoulder our crosses.

1 CORINTHIANS 1:17-18 The power of the Good News comes from the power of the cross.

EPHESIANS 2:16 Jesus' death unified all Christians.

COLOSSIANS 1:20-22 Jesus' death was a sacrifice.

COLOSSIANS 2:14-15 Jesus' death defeated Satan.

HEBREWS 12:1-4 Jesus' cross is an example for us.

Cults

MATTHEW 7:15 False teachers will come.

JOHN 14:6 Jesus is the only way to truly know God.

EPHESIANS 4:13-14; 5:12 Beware of those who teach clever lies.

1 THESSALONIANS 5:21 We should always weigh carefully what we are being taught.

2 TIMOTHY 3:2-8 Beware those who teach things that do not follow God's Word.

(See also: Occult)

Dating

2 CORINTHIANS 6:14-18 Believers should not marry unbelievers.

JAMES 4:4 Never let worldly pleasures lead you to compromise your faith.

Death

JOHN 14:19 Christ has power over death.

ROMANS 6:23 God offers eternal life to everyone.

1 CORINTHIANS 15:20-23 One day God will resurrect all believers to eternal life.

2 CORINTHIANS 5:8 Christians will be with the Lord when we die.

PHILIPPIANS 1:21-24 For Christians, even dying is gain.

1 THESSALONIANS 4:13-14 Christians who have died will one day be raised to new life.

HEBREWS 9:27-28 We all must die once, but Christ offers salvation for his followers.

JAMES 4:13-14 We don't know how long we'll live.

1 JOHN 4:17 Christians should not fear death.

REVELATION 20:14 There will be a judgment day.

REVELATION 21:4 God will destroy death.

Decisions

MATTHEW 10:34-39 Decide to love Christ above everyone.

MATTHEW 12:30 We must decide whether we will follow Jesus or not follow him.

LUKE 6:12-16 Jesus prayed before making decisions.

JAMES 1:2-8 Ask God for wisdom before making decisions.

(See also: Choices, Freedom)

Depression

JOHN 16:33 Everyone gets depressed at times.

ROMANS 4:18-22 Abraham had hope when there was no reason to hope.

EPHESIANS 1:17-18 Christians have the hope of a wonderful future through Christ.

REVELATION 21:4 God will wipe away depression.

(See also: Discouragement, Failure, Giving up, Problems)

Desires

EPHESIANS 4:22 Christians should not give in to sinful desires.

1 Peter 1:14 God's children should turn from their former, sinful desires.

1 Peter 4:2 Desire to do God's will.

1 John 2:3-6 God's children desire to obey him.

Determination
Mark 8:34-38 Determine to follow Christ.

Luke 9:62 Jesus calls us to be certain about our decision to follow him.

Devotion
Romans 12:1-2 Let your life be devoted to God.

Devotions
Mark 1:35 Jesus received strength by praying alone.

Colossians 2:6-7 Gain nourishment by reflecting on God's truth.

(See also: Bible)

Discernment
Acts 17:11 The Bible will help you discern bad teaching.

1 Corinthians 12:10 God grants discernment.

Hebrews 5:14 Mature Christians should be able to discern between right and wrong.

James 1:5 Ask God for help in discerning his will.

Discipleship

MATTHEW 28:19-20 Jesus instructed his followers to make disciples.

JOHN 13:35 Jesus' followers are known by their love.

ACTS 14:21-22 Christians should help other Christians grow.

Discipline

MATTHEW 18:15-17 There are definite steps to follow for those who are sinning.

ACTS 5:1-11 Punishment for sin may be swift and severe.

1 CORINTHIANS 5:1-5 Paul commanded punishment for blatant sin in the church.

2 CORINTHIANS 7:8-9 Punishment should lead to repentance.

EPHESIANS 6:4 Do not discipline in anger.

HEBREWS 12:5-11 Sometimes God punishes us to bring us back to himself.

REVELATION 3:19 God disciplines those he loves.

Discouragement

MATTHEW 10:16-28 Don't be discouraged by persecution.

JOHN 15:18-19 Christ's example helps us avoid discouragement from rejection.

Romans 8:35 Christ's unending love for us can help fight discouragement.

(See also: Depression, Giving up, Problems)

Discrimination
Acts 10:34 God does not discriminate among his people.

Galatians 3:28 All Christians are equally accepted by God.

Colossians 3:25 God has no favorites.

James 2:1-9 Do not discriminate against the poor.

Dishonesty
James 5:1-4 God will judge those who cheat others.

Doctrine
2 Timothy 1:13-14 Protect sound doctrine.

2 Timothy 3:16 All sound doctrine comes from Scripture.

Titus 1:6-9 Leaders in the church must have sound doctrine.

Titus 2:1 Christians should teach correct beliefs.

Doubt
Matthew 11:1-6 Jesus helped remove John's doubts.

John 20:24-29 Jesus helped remove Thomas's doubts.

HEBREWS 3:12 We must guard against unbelief in ourselves and others.

JAMES 1:5-8 Don't let doubt ruin your faith.

(See also: Faith, Trust)

Drinking
LUKE 21:34 Living in drunkenness and irresponsibility is dangerous.

ROMANS 13:11-14 Drunkenness is not fitting for a Christian.

EPHESIANS 5:18 Drunkenness can cause immoral behavior.

Drugs
1 CORINTHIANS 6:19-20 Your body is the temple of the Holy Spirit.

Embarrassment
ROMANS 1:16 We should not be embarrassed about the gospel.

GALATIANS 1:10 We should not be embarrassed about serving Christ.

Emotions
JOHN 11:35 At times Jesus experienced strong emotion.

EPHESIANS 4:31 We must make sure that our emotions do not lead us to sin.

Employment

EPHESIANS 6:6-7 Work as though Jesus were your boss.

TITUS 2:9-10 Christians should do their best at their job.

Encouragement

ACTS 9:31 The Holy Spirit comforts us.

ROMANS 15:4 The Bible encourages us.

PHILIPPIANS 2:1 Our position in Christ encourages us.

1 THESSALONIANS 4:18 We should encourage each other with thoughts of our hopeful future.

1 THESSALONIANS 5:14 Encourage those who are weak and afraid.

HEBREWS 3:13 We should encourage each other not to sin.

HEBREWS 10:24 Encourage others to show love and good deeds.

Envy

ACTS 7:9 Envy can cause you to act rashly.

ROMANS 1:29 Envy characterizes sinful people.

GALATIANS 5:26 We should not envy other Christians.

TITUS 3:3 Envy has no place in a Christian's life.

JAMES 3:14-15 Do not harbor envy.

1 PETER 2:1 Get rid of envy.

Eternal life

MATTHEW 7:13-14 Jesus is the only way to eternal life.

MATTHEW 25:46 The righteous will receive eternal life.

JOHN 3:15-16 Everyone who believes in Jesus will receive eternal life.

JOHN 5:28-29 Evil people will receive eternal punishment.

JOHN 10:10 Jesus came to give life.

JOHN 11:25 Jesus gives eternal life.

JOHN 14:6 Jesus is eternal life.

EPHESIANS 2:8-9 Eternal life cannot be earned; it is received by grace.

TITUS 1:2 Eternal life comes from God.

TITUS 3:7 Eternal life gives us hope.

(See also: Future, Heaven)

Evangelism

MATTHEW 5:14-16 Christians bring light to a spiritually dark world.

MATTHEW 9:9-13 Jesus made salvation available even to sinners.

MATTHEW 28:18-20 Jesus sent his followers to make disciples.

ACTS 1:8 The Holy Spirit gives us power to evangelize.

(See also: Witnessing)

Evil
ROMANS 1:24-28 Sometimes God allows evil to run its course.

GALATIANS 5:16-17 Our sinful nature loves evil, unlike the Holy Spirit.

EPHESIANS 4:22 Christians should put away evil from their lives.

EPHESIANS 6:12 There are spiritual forces behind evil.

Excuses
MATTHEW 25:31-46 There will be no excuses for our actions on the day of judgment.

JAMES 1:13-14 There is no excuse when we sin.

Faith
MATTHEW 8:5-13 Jesus was pleased with those who believed in him fully.

MATTHEW 9:19-26 Jesus rewards great faith.

LUKE 17:6 Even a small amount of faith can accomplish much.

ROMANS 3:28 Salvation is acquired through faith.

ROMANS 4:3-5 We are declared righteous because of our faith.

ROMANS 5:1 Faith puts us in a right relationship with God.

ROMANS 10:17 Faith comes from hearing the Word of God.

ROMANS 14:1 Accept the person who has weak faith.

EPHESIANS 4:5 Christians share one common faith.

HEBREWS 11:1 Faith is hoping in what is not seen.

HEBREWS 11:7-12 Faith should be accompanied by obedience to God.

(See also: Doubts, Trust)

Failure

LUKE 22:61-62 Though we all fail at times, we can be restored.

ROMANS 3:10 Regarding sin, we have all failed at some time or another.

(See also: Depression, Discouragement)

Family

MATTHEW 12:46-50 Those who follow God belong to his family.

LUKE 12:51-53 Christian faith is of greater importance than family.

EPHESIANS 2:19 Christians are members of God's family.

EPHESIANS 5:21-33 Husbands and wives should love each other.

EPHESIANS 6:1 Children should obey their parents.

1 TIMOTHY 3:4-5 Church leaders must have a good family life.

1 TIMOTHY 5:3-5 Families should take care of each other.

2 TIMOTHY 1:5-8 Share Christ with your family.

(See also: Home, Marriage, Parents)

Fear

ACTS 5:17-29 Faith overcomes fear.

1 JOHN 4:18 Love drives fear away.

(See also: Worry)

Foolishness

1 CORINTHIANS 1:25 The foolishness of God is wiser than man's wisdom.

Forgiveness

MATTHEW 6:14-15 We must forgive others.

MATTHEW 18:21-35 We must forgive as we have been forgiven by God.

LUKE 3:3 Turn from sin and God will forgive you.

Acts 13:38-39 Trust in Christ for forgiveness.

Colossians 3:13 Freely forgive others as God has forgiven you.

Hebrews 9:22 Jesus died so we could be forgiven.

1 John 1:8-9 God will forgive our sins as we confess them.

(See also: Confession)

Foul language
Ephesians 5:4 Foul language is not fitting for a Christian.

Colossians 4:6 Our speech should reflect our relationship with God.

1 Timothy 4:12 Our speech should be an example to others.

Freedom
John 8:30-36 Jesus can set us free from sin.

Romans 5:21 Christians are free from sin's power.

Romans 14:10-16 Don't use your freedom to lead others to sin.

Galatians 5:1 Christians are free in order to serve others.

(See also: Choices, Decisions)

Friendship

JOHN 15:13-15 Friendship is marked by sacrifice.

ACTS 9:23-29 Barnabas was a true friend to Paul.

(See also: Peer pressure, Popularity, Relationships)

Future

JOHN 3:16 Jesus came so that we could have a future of eternal life.

JOHN 14:1-4 Jesus said he was going to prepare a place for his followers.

1 CORINTHIANS 2:9 God prepares a wonderful future for his people.

(See also: Eternal life, Guidance)

Gifts

LUKE 12:48 God expects more from those who have been given more.

1 CORINTHIANS 12:1-11 The Holy Spirits equips believers with spiritual gifts.

1 TIMOTHY 4:14-16 We should use the gifts and abilities God has given us.

(See also: Using your abilities wisely)

Giving

MARK 9:41 God will reward us for giving to others.

ACTS 2:44-45 Giving should naturally flow out of our faith in Christ.

1 TIMOTHY 6:17-19 Wealthy people should give generously.

HEBREWS 13:16 God is pleased with our gifts.

1 JOHN 3:17 Giving reflects God's love.

Giving up
1 CORINTHIANS 9:24-27 Discipline yourself for endurance.

GALATIANS 6:9-10 Never get tired of doing right.

PHILIPPIANS 3:12-14 Never give up the race of obedience to Christ.

2 TIMOTHY 2:3-13 Don't give up even when you are suffering.

(See also: Depression, Discouragement)

Goals
PHILIPPIANS 3:12-20 Following Christ should be our ultimate goal.

JAMES 4:13-16 Make sure your goals please God.

God
MATTHEW 6:9 God is our father.

LUKE 1:37 God is all-powerful.

JOHN 4:24 God is spirit.

ROMANS 11:33 God is all-knowing.

EPHESIANS 1:17 God is knowable.

1 TIMOTHY 4:10 God is living.

1 TIMOTHY 6:15 God is King of kings.

JAMES 4:8 God will draw close to us.

JAMES 4:12 God is judge.

1 JOHN 4:16 God is love.

REVELATION 1:8 God is almighty.

God's will
MATTHEW 1:18-25 Follow God's will even if you don't understand it.

ACTS 16:6-7 God directs events in our life.

PHILIPPIANS 2:13-16 God wants to help you do his will.

JAMES 1:2-5 God gives wisdom for making decisions.

(See also: Bible)

Gospel/Good News
MATTHEW 28:18-19 Christians should tell others about the gospel.

LUKE 24:46-47 The gospel is for everyone.

JOHN 1:12 People should respond to the gospel with faith.

ROMANS 1:16 The gospel is powerful.

1 CORINTHIANS 15:1-5 The gospel is that Jesus died for our sins and rose again.

1 THESSALONIANS 1:4-5 Believing the gospel brings a change to life.

Gossip
ROMANS 1:29 Gossiping is wicked.

2 THESSALONIANS 3:11-12 God hates gossiping.

1 TIMOTHY 5:13 Gossip should have no place among Christians.

TITUS 3:2 Don't speak evil of anyone.

(See also: Communication, Lying)

Government
ROMANS 13:1 God gives authority to those in government.

TITUS 3:1 Christians should obey the government.

Grace
EPHESIANS 1:7-8 God's grace makes salvation possible.

EPHESIANS 2:8-9 God accepts us by his grace.

1 PETER 1:13 God's grace gives us hope.

Greed
MATTHEW 26:14-15 Greed caused Judas to betray Jesus.

EPHESIANS 5:3 Christians should not be greedy.

EPHESIANS 5:5 People who are full of greed will not enter heaven.

TITUS 1:7 Leaders of the church must not be greedy.

2 PETER 2:15 Greed causes some to use religion to get rich.

(See also: Materialism, Money, Possessions)

Grief

MATTHEW 5:4 God promises to comfort those who grieve.

JOHN 14:16 God's Holy Spirit is our Comforter.

JOHN 16:33 Jesus has overcome the world's troubles.

ACTS 9:31 The Holy Spirit comforts us.

ROMANS 15:4 The Scriptures encourage us.

2 CORINTHIANS 1:3-11 God comforts those who grieve.

REVELATION 21:3-4 One day all grief will end.

(See also: Sorrow)

Guidance

MATTHEW 2:13-15 Sometimes God uses unusual ways to guide us.

ACTS 8:26-37 Sometimes God guides us to help others.

(See also: Future, God's will, Prayer)

Guilt

Romans 3:9-12 Everyone is guilty of sin.

Romans 3:23-24 Jesus Christ takes away all guilt.

1 Timothy 1:12-17 God can forgive even the most wicked of sinners.

(See also: Confession, Forgiveness)

Happiness

Matthew 5:3-12 Jesus told his followers how to be truly happy.

1 Timothy 6:6-10 Contentedness and sincerity in our faith brings much happiness.

(See also: Contentment)

Hatred

Matthew 10:22 Followers of Jesus will be hated.

John 15:18 Many in the world hate Jesus.

Romans 12:9 Christians should hate evil.

Colossians 3:8 Christians need to get rid of their own hatred.

1 John 3:15 Those who hate fellow Christians are murderers at heart.

(See also: Anger, Revenge)

Heart

Matthew 5:8 Those who have pure hearts will see God.

LUKE 6:45 Words and actions reflect what is in the heart.

Heaven

MATTHEW 5:17-20 Actions on earth affect position in heaven.

MATTHEW 7:13-14 The road and gateway to heaven are very narrow.

LUKE 13:29 People from all over the world will be together in heaven.

JOHN 14:2-3 Jesus said he was preparing a place in heaven for his followers.

2 CORINTHIANS 5:2 Our earthly bodies will be made complete in heaven.

PHILIPPIANS 1:23 We can look forward to heaven.

COLOSSIANS 3:1-5 Christians should look forward to heaven.

REVELATION 7:17 God is the focus of attention in heaven.

REVELATION 22:3-4 There will not be any evil or sadness in heaven.

REVELATION 22:5 God will be heaven's light.

(See also: Eternal life)

Hell

MATTHEW 7:22-23 Even some who do good deeds will end up in hell.

MATTHEW 8:12 Hell is a place of weeping.

MATTHEW 25:41 Hell was prepared for Satan and demons.

LUKE 16:19-31 Hell is real and eternal.

ACTS 4:12 Jesus Christ is the only one who can save us from hell.

ROMANS 1:18-20 Wicked people will receive punishment.

ROMANS 2:1-9 God will punish those who sin.

2 THESSALONIANS 1:7-9 Hell is eternal separation from God.

2 PETER 2:4-9 God will punish those who do not turn from their sin.

JUDE 1:7 Hell is a place of eternal fire.

REVELATION 1:17-18 Jesus holds the keys to hell.

REVELATION 20:14 Hell is described as a lake of fire.

REVELATION 21:8 Those who do not believe in God are destined for hell.

Holy

JOHN 17:17 God makes us holy as he teaches us his truth.

1 PETER 1:15 Christians must be holy.

REVELATION 4:8 God is holy and worthy of praise.

Holy Spirit

MATTHEW 12:31-32 Never sin against the Holy Spirit.

JOHN 3:6-8 The Holy Spirit gives us new life.

JOHN 14:26 The Holy Spirit teaches us.

JOHN 16:13 The Holy Spirit guides us.

ACTS 1:8 The Holy Spirit empowers us to be witnesses.

ROMANS 8:2 The Holy Spirit helps us live as Christians.

ROMANS 8:11 The Holy Spirit lives within us.

ROMANS 15:16 The Holy Spirit can make us pure and pleasing to God.

1 CORINTHIANS 2:10 The Holy Spirit opens our eyes to truth about God.

2 CORINTHIANS 5:16-17 The Holy Spirit makes us new people.

TITUS 3:5 The Holy Spirit gives us new life as our sins are removed.

Home

ACTS 5:42 We should study the Bible at home.

EPHESIANS 6:1-4 Faith is needed at home.

2 JOHN 1:10 Don't open your home to false teachers.

(See also: Family)

186

Homosexuality

ROMANS 1:18-27 Homosexual practices are sinful.

1 CORINTHIANS 6:9-10 Homosexual behavior has no place among Christians.

Honesty

MATTHEW 5:37 Christians should be known by their simple and honest promises.

MATTHEW 15:18-20 Lies come from an evil heart.

EPHESIANS 4:25 Christians should put away dishonesty from their lives.

1 THESSALONIANS 2:4-5 Be honest in witnessing.

JAMES 5:12 Be straightforward and honest in your promises.

(See also: Integrity, Lying)

Hope

ROMANS 8:28 Christians always have hope.

ROMANS 15:13 Christians have hope through the power of the Holy Spirit.

1 CORINTHIANS 6:14 Jesus' resurrection gives us hope.

1 CORINTHIANS 15:19-20 Christians have eternal hope in Christ.

1 CORINTHIANS 15:54-58 Christians can look forward to the day when death is eliminated.

TITUS 1:1-2 We have confidence of eternal life.

HEBREWS 6:13-20 We can find hope in God's promises.

HEBREWS 11:1 Faith is the confident assurance that what we hope for will happen.

Hospitality

MATTHEW 25:34-40 Christians should take care of those in need.

MARK 9:41 Hospitality brings heavenly reward.

ROMANS 12:13 Christians should be hospitable.

HEBREWS 13:2 Christians should be hospitable even to people they do not know well.

1 PETER 4:9-11 Be cheerful about being hospitable.

3 JOHN 1:5-8 Hospitality reflects God's love.

Humility

MATTHEW 3:11-12 John the Baptist was humble.

LUKE 18:14 God will exalt the humble.

PHILIPPIANS 2:1-11 Be humble in dealing with others.

JAMES 4:10 Humble yourself before God.

1 PETER 5:5 Be humble and serve others.

Hypocrisy

MATTHEW 23:13 Hypocrites try to keep others from entering the Kingdom of God.

MATTHEW 23:27-28 Hypocrites try to look good though they have evil hearts.

LUKE 12:1-2 Beware of hypocrisy in your life.

LUKE 20:46-47 God will punish hypocrisy.

1 PETER 2:1 Get rid of hypocrisy in your life.

Idolatry

LUKE 16:13 Christians cannot serve both God and the things of this world.

COLOSSIANS 3:5 Being greedy for things of this life is idolatry.

Immorality

1 CORINTHIANS 5:9-11 Stay away from immoral Christians.

1 CORINTHIANS 6:19-20 Sexual immorality defiles our body, the temple of the Holy Spirit.

EPHESIANS 4:17-19 Immorality should have no place among Christians.

(See also: Sex/Sexual sin)

Insult

LUKE 6:22 God will bless Christians who are insulted because of their faith.

1 PETER 3:9 Do not repay insults to others.

Integrity

PHILIPPIANS 3:17 Be an example to others by your integrity.

TITUS 1:7 Leaders in the church should be full of integrity.

TITUS 2:7 Maintain integrity in teaching others.

(See also: Honesty, Lying)

Intimidation

JOHN 16:33 Jesus' victory over the world can give us courage.

ACTS 4:31 God will help us be bold.

1 CORINTHIANS 16:13 Be courageous and firm in your faith.

EPHESIANS 6:19-20 We can pray for courage.

HEBREWS 4:16 Christians can boldly bring their requests to God.

Jealousy

MATTHEW 18:1-4 Don't be jealous of the greatness of others.

JOHN 3:26-30 A proper view of God's role for us can help remove jealousy.

ACTS 7:9 Jealousy can cause rash behavior.

ACTS 13:44-48 Never be jealous of others who do God's work.

ROMANS 13:13-14 Don't let jealousy control you.

GALATIANS 5:26 We should not be jealous of other Christians.

PHILIPPIANS 1:15-18 Some people even do good things out of jealousy.

TITUS 3:3-5 Jealousy has no place in a Christian's life.

Jesus Christ

MARK 1:27 Jesus has authority over demons.

LUKE 1:35 Jesus is the Son of God.

JOHN 1:1-5 Jesus is God.

JOHN 4:25-26 Jesus is the Messiah.

JOHN 5:22 Jesus will judge all people.

JOHN 10:10 Jesus gives life.

JOHN 10:11 Jesus is the Good Shepherd.

JOHN 14:6 Jesus is the only way to God.

ACTS 3:15 Jesus is the author of life.

1 CORINTHIANS 1:21-24 Jesus is the wisdom of God.

EPHESIANS 5:23 Jesus is the head of the church.

PHILIPPIANS 2:9-10 Jesus is the highest authority.

COLOSSIANS 1:15-16 God created and sustains the world through Christ.

2 Timothy 2:13 Jesus is faithful.

Titus 2:13 Jesus is coming again.

Hebrews 4:15 Jesus is sinless.

Hebrews 7:26 Jesus is holy.

Revelation 15:3 Jesus is the King of the ages.

Revelation 21:22 Jesus is the Lamb of God.

Judgment
Matthew 12:36 God will judge the words we speak.

John 7:21-24 God does not judge by appearances.

Romans 14:10 God will judge Christians.

2 Corinthians 5:10 Christ will judge Christians for their actions.

Hebrews 9:27 We are destined to die once and face judgment.

Revelation 20:11-15 People whose names are in the Book of Life will enter heaven.

Justice
Romans 3:25-26 God is just in his judgment of people.

Kindness
Ephesians 4:32 Christians should be kind to each other.

1 THESSALONIANS 5:15 Be kind to people who treat you wrongly.

2 TIMOTHY 2:24 Choose to be kind rather than to argue.

2 PETER 1:5-7 Kindness and love can be cultivated.

Kingdom of God/Heaven

MATTHEW 3:1-2 You must turn from sin before you can enter God's Kingdom.

MATTHEW 5:1-19 Jesus describes members of God's Kingdom.

MATTHEW 5:19 Obeying God's commands yields great rewards in his Kingdom.

MATTHEW 5:20 Only righteous people will enter God's Kingdom.

MATTHEW 7:21 God's Kingdom is open to those who do his will.

MATTHEW 9:35-36 God's Kingdom is characterized by healing.

MATTHEW 13:44-45 Entering God's Kingdom costs us everything.

MATTHEW 18:2-3 God's Kingdom is reserved for the humble.

MATTHEW 18:23-35 No one deserves God's Kingdom.

LUKE 17:20-21 God's Kingdom is within our hearts.

LUKE 21:25-31 God's Kingdom will fully arrive in the future.

JOHN 3:3 Only those who are spiritually reborn can enter God's Kingdom.

ACTS 14:22 Entering God's Kingdom is not easy.

ACTS 28:31 Christians should tell others about the Kingdom of God.

ROMANS 14:17 God's Kingdom affects our lives.

1 CORINTHIANS 4:20 God's Kingdom is powerful.

EPHESIANS 5:5 No immoral person will be allowed into God's Kingdom.

COLOSSIANS 1:13 Christians are members of God's Kingdom.

1 THESSALONIANS 2:12 Christians' lives should reflect their membership in God's Kingdom.

1 THESSALONIANS 2:12 God calls people into his Kingdom.

HEBREWS 12:28 God's Kingdom cannot be shaken.

REVELATION 11:15 God's Kingdom will one day be fully consummated.

Laziness

1 THESSALONIANS 5:14 Encourage lazy people to work.

2 THESSALONIANS 3:10 Lazy people should not be allowed to be freeloaders.

Leadership

MATTHEW 20:26-28 Leaders must be servants.

ROMANS 13:1-4 Leaders should be obeyed.

TITUS 1:7 God has given specific qualifications for church leaders.

HEBREWS 13:17 Leaders give an account to God for their actions.

Life

JOHN 3:3 People must be reborn spiritually to enter heaven.

JOHN 10:10 Jesus came to give life in all its fullness.

EPHESIANS 4:1 We should live lives worthy of our Christian calling.

PHILIPPIANS 1:21 Following Christ is the reason to live.

COLOSSIANS 3:17 We should live as representatives of Jesus Christ.

Loneliness

MATTHEW 28:20 God will always be with us.

MARK 15:33-39 Christ knows what it is like to be lonely.

Lord's Supper

MATTHEW 26:26-29 Jesus celebrated the Lord's Supper with his disciples.

1 CORINTHIANS 10:16-18 Celebrating the Lord's Supper together should unify believers.

1 CORINTHIANS 11:23-26 The Lord's Supper remind us of Jesus' death.

Love

MATTHEW 5:38-42 Christlike love does not repay evil for evil.

MATTHEW 5:43-44 Love your enemies.

MATTHEW 23:37-39 Jesus loves his people.

MARK 12:29-30 Loving God is the most important commandment.

JOHN 13:34 Christians must love each other.

ROMANS 8:35-39 We cannot be separated from Christ's love.

ROMANS 12:9 Love must be genuine.

1 CORINTHIANS 13:4-8 God has described real love for us.

EPHESIANS 3:18 God's love for us is beyond our understanding.

PHILIPPIANS 1:3-8 Paul dearly loved the Philippians.

1 PETER 4:8 Love makes up for many offenses.

1 JOHN 4:16 God is love.

2 JOHN 1:5 We must be known for our love.

Loyalty

MATTHEW 6:24 We cannot divide our loyalty.

HEBREWS 13:4 There must be loyalty in marriage.

Lust

MATTHEW 5:28 Dwelling on lustful thoughts is sinful.

COLOSSIANS 3:5 Christians should not give in to lust.

1 THESSALONIANS 4:3-5 Christians should avoid lust.

1 PETER 4:3 Lust and immorality characterize the ungodly.

Lying

MATTHEW 15:18-20 Lying comes from the heart.

(See also: Dishonesty, Honesty, Integrity)

Marriage

MATTHEW 19:3-6 Marriage is a lifelong commitment.

MARK 10:2-12 Two people become one through marriage.

MARK 12:25 Angels do not marry.

1 CORINTHIANS 7:2-5 Married partners should look after each other's needs.

1 CORINTHIANS 7:39 Married partners are united to each other for life.

1 PETER 3:1-6 Christians can be witnesses to their non-Christian spouse.

(See also: Family, Home, Sexual sin)

Materialism

MATTHEW 4:8-11 Satan can tempt us with material things.

MATTHEW 19:21-30 Don't put things before your love for God.

COLOSSIANS 3:1-5 Focusing on heaven can help us avoid materialism.

1 JOHN 2:17 Don't live for things that don't last.

REVELATION 18:9-14 Material things won't last.

(See also: Greed, Money, Possessions)

Mercy

MATTHEW 5:7 People who show mercy to others will receive mercy.

LUKE 6:36 We should imitate God's mercy.

1 TIMOTHY 1:2 We can pray for God's mercy upon people.

Messiah

Mark 8:27-29 Eventually Jesus' disciples knew he was the Messiah.

Mark 14:61-62 Jesus admitted that he was the Messiah and that he will come again.

John 4:25-42 Jesus claimed to be the Messiah.

Mind

Matthew 5:27 Guard your mind against lustful thoughts.

Romans 12:2 A Christian's thoughts should be holy.

1 Corinthians 2:6-16 God grants wisdom to his followers.

Philippians 4:8 We should focus our minds on things that strengthen our faith.

Money

Matthew 6:19 Never value your money more than God.

Mark 10:21-24 Trust and love God, not money.

Luke 16:13 You cannot serve both God and money.

Acts 2:42-45 Christians should share their resources with those in need.

1 Timothy 3:3 Christians should not be lovers of money.

1 TIMOTHY 6:5 Stay away from money-hungry preachers.

1 TIMOTHY 6:10 The love of money is a root of all kinds of evil.

1 TIMOTHY 6:17-19 We should look to God, not money, for security.

HEBREWS 13:5 Do not love money.

JAMES 2:1-9 Be careful to treat rich and poor equally.

JAMES 5:1-6 Money is only temporary.

(See also: Greed, Materialism, Possessions)

Music
COLOSSIANS 3:16 We should make music for God's glory.

Obedience
MATTHEW 1:18-25 Be more concerned about obeying God than pleasing people.

MATTHEW 2:13-15, 19-23 Obey God even when you don't understand.

MATTHEW 4:18-22 Obey Christ when he calls to you.

MATTHEW 7:21-29 Obedience is the true test of whether we are God's followers.

LUKE 1:38 Mary was obedient to God.

LUKE 11:28 People who obey God's Word will be blessed.

John 14:21 Obeying God shows your love for him.

Romans 13:1-4 Christians should obey the government.

Ephesians 6:1 Children should obey their parents.

Hebrews 11:7 Others may scoff at your obedience.

1 John 2:3 Christians obey God.

(See also: God's will)

Occult
Acts 19:18-20 Believers in Ephesus burned their books of witchcraft.

(See also: Cults)

Opportunities
Acts 3:12-16 Look for opportunities to glorify God.

Ephesians 2:10 Use your opportunities to live for Christ.

Philippians 1:12-14 Turn your troubles into opportunities.

Pain
Matthew 5:4 God promises to comfort those who mourn.

John 14:16 God's Holy Spirit is our Comforter.

1 Thessalonians 4:18 Christians should comfort each other.

REVELATION 21:3-4 One day all pain will end.

Parents

EPHESIANS 6:1 Obey your parents.

EPHESIANS 6:2-3 Honor your parents and be blessed.

EPHESIANS 6:4 Parents should not simply frustrate their children.

COLOSSIANS 3:20 Children must obey their parents.

(See also: Authority)

Partying

MATTHEW 24:42-51 Don't live wildly and abandon your responsibilities toward God.

ROMANS 13:11-14 Don't give your life over to wild parties and drunkenness.

1 CORINTHIANS 10:31 Glorify God in all you do, and don't cause others to stumble.

(See also: Peer pressure)

Patience

LUKE 15:11-24 God patiently waits for his lost children to return to him.

ROMANS 8:24-30 We must be patient as we wait for God's plan to unfold.

1 CORINTHIANS 13:4 Love is patient.

GALATIANS 5:22 Patience is evidence of the Holy Spirit working in our lives.

EPHESIANS 4:2 Be patient with each other.

2 THESSALONIANS 1:4-5 Patience helps you endure suffering.

HEBREWS 11:13-16 We must be patient and wait to receive all that God has promised.

Peace

MATTHEW 5:23-26 Make peace with others quickly.

JOHN 14:27 The peace Jesus gives is different than the world's peace.

ROMANS 5:1 Jesus gives us peace.

1 CORINTHIANS 1:3 We can pray for God's peace for others.

GALATIANS 5:22 Peace is evidence of the Holy Spirit working in our lives.

PHILIPPIANS 4:4-7 We can have peace through prayer.

Peer pressure

LUKE 6:22-23 God will bless us when we are mocked for our faith.

ROMANS 1:30-32 We need to beware of being influenced by sinful people.

ROMANS 12:1-2 Don't desire to copy the world's ways.

JAMES 1:2-4 Life's pressures can strengthen us.

(See also: Conformity, Popularity)

Persistence

LUKE 18:1-8 Be persistent in prayer.

1 CORINTHIANS 9:24-27 We ought to be persistent in our striving to live for God.

GALATIANS 6:7-10 Be persistent in doing good.

EPHESIANS 6:18 Be persistent in prayers for others.

PHILIPPIANS 3:12-14 Keep striving to live for Christ.

Popularity

MATTHEW 10:32-33 Don't let your concern for popularity make you ashamed of Christ.

JOHN 15:18-19 Following Christ will guarantee that some people will hate you.

2 CORINTHIANS 4:4 Satan makes his followers hate Christians.

JAMES 4:4 God doesn't want us to be popular with everyone.

1 JOHN 2:15-17 Believers must stay away from some popular activities.

(See also: Conformity, Peer pressure)

Possessions

MATTHEW 19:16-22 Don't let possessions keep you from following Christ.

ACTS 2:42-45 Christians should be generous in sharing their possessions.

JAMES 2:1-9 Don't show favoritism toward wealthy people.

(See also: Greed, Materialism, Money)

Power

ACTS 1:8 Christians receive power from the Holy Spirit.

EPHESIANS 6:17 God's Word is a powerful weapon.

HEBREWS 1:1-4 Jesus sustains the universe by his powerful command.

JAMES 5:16 Earnest prayer from a righteous person has powerful results.

1 JOHN 5:4-5 God gives Christians power to overcome the world.

Praise

(See: Worship)

Prayer

MATTHEW 6:6 Prayer should not be done for show.

MATTHEW 6:9-13 Jesus taught his disciples how to pray.

MATTHEW 7:7-12 We must be persistent in prayer.

MATTHEW 21:21-22 We can pray with confidence that God is able to answer our requests.

LUKE 18:9-14 Pray with an attitude of humility.

JOHN 16:23-24 Pray with confidence in Jesus' name.

EPHESIANS 6:18 Pray all the time.

2 THESSALONIANS 1:11 Pray for others.

JAMES 1:6 Pray without doubting.

JAMES 4:3 Pray with right motives.

1 JOHN 5:14-15 Pray according to God's will.

(See also: Choices, Decisions, Guidance)

Prejudice

MARK 6:1-6 Prejudice makes us blind to God's truth.

LUKE 10:25-37 Prejudice keeps us from helping others.

ACTS 10:34-43 Jesus died for everyone.

GALATIANS 3:28-29 All Christians are equally accepted by God.

EPHESIANS 2:11-16 Christ has made it possible to remove prejudice.

Pride

MATTHEW 11:20-26 Pride keeps people from finding Christ.

LUKE 18:9-14 Pride cuts us off from God and others.

ROMANS 3:27 There is no place for proud boasting in the Christian life.

1 CORINTHIANS 1:26-31 God chose to reveal himself to the humble, not the proud.

GALATIANS 5:22-26 Pride is not compatible with the fruit of the Spirit.

JAMES 4:6 God opposes the proud.

(See also: Self-esteem)

Problems

MATTHEW 11:27-30 Jesus offers rest for the weary.

ROMANS 8:28 God can bring good from any problem.

PHILIPPIANS 1:29-30 We should view suffering for Christ as a privilege.

PHILIPPIANS 3:7-11 Our struggles allow us to share in Christ's suffering.

(See also: Depression, Discouragement, Failure, Stress, Suffering, Trials)

Procrastination

MATTHEW 25:1-13 Do not procrastinate in securing your relationship with God.

2 CORINTHIANS 6:2 Today is the day to be saved.

REVELATION 10:6 No one can procrastinate forever.

Prophecy

MATTHEW 7:21-23 Claiming to prophesy does not make you right before God.

ACTS 2:17-18 The Holy Spirit allows believers to prophesy.

1 CORINTHIANS 14:1-5 Prophecy is a spiritual gift.

1 THESSALONIANS 5:20 We should listen to God's messages.

2 PETER 1:20-21 True prophets speak God's words.

(See also: Teaching)

Purity

MATTHEW 5:8 The pure in heart will see God.

MATTHEW 5:27-30 Purity begins in the heart.

MATTHEW 23:25-28 Outward purity cannot substitute for inner purity.

JOHN 17:17 Purity comes from God.

EPHESIANS 5:1-4 Purity ought to mark believers' lives.

PHILIPPIANS 3:7-11 Give up what hinders purity.

PHILIPPIANS 4:8 Our minds should think about things that are pure.

1 JOHN 3:1-3 One day our purity will be like Christ's.

(See also: Marriage, Sexual sin)

Questions

LUKE 7:18-23 Christ does not rebuke us for asking sincere questions.

LUKE 21:12-15 We need not be afraid when questioned about our faith.

1 PETER 3:15 We should be ready with answers when questioned about our faith.

Rapture

(See: Second Coming of Christ)

Rejection

MATTHEW 13:53-58 Jesus was rejected in his hometown.

LUKE 15:11-24 God does not reject repentant sinners.

JOHN 6:58-66 Jesus was rejected by many of his followers.

ROMANS 1:18-32 Rejecting God allows sin to run wild.

Relationships

JOHN 14:19-21 Our relationship with God is made possible through Jesus Christ.

1 CORINTHIANS 11:2-12 Humility strengthens family relationships.

2 CORINTHIANS 6:14-18 Our relationships should not compromise our faith.

EPHESIANS 2:21-22 We are united with all believers in God's family.

2 TIMOTHY 2:11-13 Christians have a deep relationship with Christ.

PHILEMON 1:12-14 Often we can build good relationships in bad situations.

1 JOHN 3:1-3 Our relationship with Christ makes us children of God.

(See also: Friendships, Marriage)

Repentance

LUKE 3:7-8 Changed lives give evidence of true repentance.

LUKE 13:3-5 Unless we repent of our sins, we will perish.

LUKE 15:7 Angels rejoice when a sinner repents.

LUKE 17:4 Forgive those who repent of wrongs done to you.

ACTS 2:38 Repentance results in forgiveness and the coming of the Holy Spirit.

2 CORINTHIANS 7:9-10 God can use difficulties to encourage us to repent.

2 PETER 3:9 God would like everyone to repent and believe.

(See also: Confession)

RON BALL

Reputation
ROMANS 16:19 The Christians in Rome had a reputation for obedience.

2 CORINTHIANS 8:18-24 Guard your reputation.

2 CORINTHIANS 12:11-16 Stand up for your reputation.

COLOSSIANS 4:5 Maintain a good reputation among non-Christians.

TITUS 1:5-9 Elders must have a good reputation.

Respect
EPHESIANS 5:33 Husbands and wives should respect each other.

1 TIMOTHY 3:4 Those in leadership should have respectful children.

1 PETER 2:17 Show respect to all people.

(See also: Authority)

Responsibility
MATTHEW 25:14-30 Responsible people are faithful with what they have been given.

MATTHEW 27:23-26 God holds us accountable.

JOHN 3:18-19 People are responsible for their decision about Christ.

ACTS 6:1-7 Responsible people know their abilities and limitations.

1 TIMOTHY 3:1-16 Leaders have strict responsibilities.

JAMES 1:13-15 People are responsible for their own actions.

Rest

MATTHEW 11:28-30 Jesus promises to give us rest from our burdens.

HEBREWS 4:9-11 God promises one day to give us rest.

REVELATION 14:13 Heaven will be a place of rest.

Resurrection

MATTHEW 28:5-10 Christ's resurrection is a historical fact.

JOHN 6:38-40 Jesus promised to raise his followers.

JOHN 11:24-26 Everyone will be resurrected one day.

ROMANS 6:3-11 We will experience resurrection.

1 CORINTHIANS 15:12-21 Jesus' resurrection is the foundation of Christianity.

1 CORINTHIANS 15:51-53 Our resurrected bodies will be eternal bodies.

Revenge

MATTHEW 5:38-48 Christians should pay back evil with good.

ROMANS 12:19 Leave revenge in God's hands.

1 THESSALONIANS 5:15 Desire for revenge is not compatible with the Christian life.

I PETER 2:21-23 Jesus is our example of how to handle insults and suffering.

I PETER 3:8-9 Be tender and humble.

(See also: Anger, Hatred)

Righteous/righteousness

ROMANS 3:10-18 We are not righteous by ourselves.

ROMANS 4:18-25 Righteousness is not attained by works.

GALATIANS 3:11-21 Trying to keep the law cannot make us righteous.

EPHESIANS 6:14 Our God-given righteousness is armor against Satan's attacks.

PHILIPPIANS 3:9 We become righteous through faith in Christ.

2 TIMOTHY 3:16 Studying God's Word helps us grow in righteousness.

I PETER 2:24 Righteousness ought to characterize each believer's life.

Sadness

(See: Grief, Sorrow)

Salvation

MATTHEW 19:25-26 Salvation is by God's grace alone.

JOHN 1:12-13 Those who receive salvation become God's children.

JOHN 3:1-16 Salvation is a work of the Holy Spirit in a person's life.

JOHN 14:6 Jesus is the way to salvation.

JOHN 17:1-5 Salvation involves knowing the Father through his Son, Jesus Christ.

ACTS 2:37-38 Receiving salvation means we must turn from our sins.

ROMANS 3:8 Jesus died for our sins.

ROMANS 3:23 No one deserves salvation.

ROMANS 6:23 Salvation cannot be earned; it is a gift of God.

ROMANS 8:38-39 Salvation is eternal.

ROMANS 10:8-10 Receiving salvation is simple and personal.

EPHESIANS 2:1-9 Salvation is by God's grace alone.

PHILIPPIANS 3:4-11 No one is good enough to be saved.

COLOSSIANS 1:13-14 Salvation means being rescued from Satan's dominion.

1 PETER 1:18-19 Our salvation was obtained by Jesus' blood.

Satan

MATTHEW 4:1-11 Satan even tempted Jesus.

JOHN 8:44 Satan is completely evil.

EPHESIANS 2:1-2 Satan is the temporary ruler over this world.

EPHESIANS 6:12 Satan and his demons are spiritual.

JAMES 4:1-10 Believers have the authority to resist Satan.

1 PETER 5:8 Satan is an enemy to Christians.

1 JOHN 3:7-8 Jesus destroyed Satan's work with his death on the cross.

REVELATION 20:10 Satan is a defeated enemy.

Second Coming of Christ

MATTHEW 24:36 We do not know when Jesus will return.

MARK 13:26-27 Christ's return will be unmistakable.

LUKE 12:35-40 Christ's return will be joyous for those who are ready.

JOHN 12:37-50 Christ's second coming will be a time of judgment on unbelievers.

JOHN 14:1-3 At Christ's second coming we will be with him forever.

ACTS 1:10-11 We have the promise that Christ will one day return.

1 CORINTHIANS 15:51-57 When Christ returns, believers will be resurrected into new bodies.

1 THESSALONIANS 4:16 Christ's return will be visible and glorious.

1 THESSALONIANS 4:16-17 At Christ's return, Christians who are dead and alive will rise to meet him.

1 PETER 4:7-8 Continue to serve God as you await the Second Coming.

2 PETER 3:8-13 Patiently await Christ's return.

REVELATION 22:20-21 Jesus is coming soon.

Self-esteem

MATTHEW 18:10-14 God rejoices over our decision to come to him.

LUKE 12:4-12 We are of great value to God.

JOHN 3:16 God gave his Son for us.

ROMANS 8:38-39 Nothing can separate us from Christ's love.

ROMANS 12:3-8 We should hold an honest evaluation of ourselves among God's people.

ROMANS 13:9 We should love others as we love ourselves.

2 CORINTHIANS 10:12-18 We should only boast in what God has done.

GALATIANS 6:3-5 We should not overestimate ourselves.

(See also: Pride)

Serving others

MATTHEW 20:28 We should imitate Christ's example and serve others.

JOHN 13:3-5 Jesus shows service by his example.

PHILIPPIANS 2:5-8 Serve others as Jesus did.

(See also: Caring, Compassion)

Sex/Sexual sin

MATTHEW 5:27-30 Sexual sin begins in the mind.

ROMANS 1:24-27 Homosexuality and lesbianism are sins.

1 CORINTHIANS 6:13-20 Sex is a powerful bond not meant to be taken lightly.

EPHESIANS 5:1-3 Sexual immorality has no place among Christians.

COLOSSIANS 3:5 We are to have nothing to do with sexual immorality.

1 THESSALONIANS 4:1-8 God wants us to live in holiness, not lustful passion.

HEBREWS 13:4 Sex in marriage is honorable and pure.

(See also: Dating, Homosexuality, Marriage, Peer pressure, Purity, Temptation)

Sickness

MATTHEW 4:23-25 Jesus can heal sickness.

MATTHEW 25:34-40 Believers ought to care for the sick.

2 CORINTHIANS 12:7-10 Paul had an infirmity that God would not remove.

Sin
MATTHEW 5:27-28 Sin begins in the mind.

MATTHEW 25:45 Refusing to help when you are able is sin.

MARK 2:1-12 Jesus has the authority to forgive sins.

ROMANS 3:23 All people have sinned.

ROMANS 6:23 Sin leads to eternal death.

ROMANS 8:1-2 Jesus took the penalty of our sin on himself.

JAMES 1:15 Sin comes from allowing our evil desires to influence us.

JAMES 4:17 We can sin by avoiding something we should do.

1 JOHN 1:8-9 God can forgive our sins.

(See also: Conscience, Consequences, Temptation)

Singleness
MATTHEW 19:12 Some people remain single to work for God's Kingdom.

1 CORINTHIANS 7:7-8 God gives some people the gift of singleness.

1 Corinthians 7:25-31 Sometimes singleness is best in certain situations.

1 Corinthians 7:32-35 Single people have more time to focus on service for God.

Sorrow

Matthew 5:4 God promises comfort to those who experience sorrow.

2 Corinthians 7:10-11 God may use sorrow to point out sin and draw us back to him.

1 Thessalonians 4:13-18 Christians can look to their hopeful future to help alleviate sorrow.

Revelation 21:3-4 Sorrow will not exist in God's Kingdom.

(See also: Grief)

Soul

Matthew 10:28 People cannot destroy your soul.

Matthew 22:36-40 We are to love God with our whole being—heart, soul, and mind.

Mark 8:34-38 It is of no value to gain the world but lose your soul.

Spiritual gifts

Romans 12:3-8 God expects us to use our gifts.

1 Corinthians 12:4-11 God gives us our spiritual gifts.

EPHESIANS 4:11-13 Spiritual gifts build up the body of Christ.

HEBREWS 2:4 God distributes spiritual gifts according to his will.

Stress
ROMANS 8:31-39 God is always with us.

2 CORINTHIANS 4:8-12 God is with us during stressful times.

PHILIPPIANS 4:4-9 Praying about everything helps us not to worry.

Submission
MATTHEW 26:36-44 Christ is the perfect example of submission to the Father's will.

LUKE 14:27 Following Christ requires submission to him.

1 CORINTHIANS 11:2-16 Harmonious relationships require submission to authority.

EPHESIANS 5:21-33 Marriage calls for mutual submission.

JAMES 4:7-10 Submit to God.

(See also: Obedience)

Suffering
MATTHEW 16:21-26 Christ's followers will face suffering.

ROMANS 8:18-21 The curse of sin has brought suffering.

2 CORINTHIANS 1:3-7 Our suffering helps us comfort others who are suffering.

2 CORINTHIANS 4:17-18 Our suffering will end in glory.

HEBREWS 2:11-18 Jesus can help us in our suffering.

1 PETER 2:21-24 We should imitate Christ's response to suffering.

REVELATION 21:4 There will be no suffering in Christ's Kingdom.

(See also: Problems, Trials, Trust)

Teaching

2 TIMOTHY 2:2 Christians are to teach each other God's truth.

2 TIMOTHY 2:24-26 We should be patient as we teach God's truth to others.

TITUS 2:1-15 Christians should teach each other how to live for God.

(See also: Witnessing)

Temptation

MATTHEW 4:1-11 Jesus experienced temptation and overcame it.

1 CORINTHIANS 10:13 God will provide a way of escape from every temptation.

1 TIMOTHY 6:11-12 Paul encouraged Timothy to run from temptation and pursue godliness.

2 TIMOTHY 2:22 We are to run from temptation and pursue good things.

HEBREWS 2:16-18 Jesus can help us when we are tempted.

HEBREWS 4:15-16 Christ can help us, for he, too, has faced temptation.

JAMES 1:13-15 God never tempts people to sin.

(See also: Sin)

Thankfulness

LUKE 17:11-18 Always thank God for his blessings.

ACTS 3:7-11 Thankfulness brings praise to God.

EPHESIANS 2:4-10 Be thankful for salvation and God's grace.

PHILIPPIANS 4:6 We should thank God for all he has done.

COLOSSIANS 3:15-17 Our life should be characterized by thankfulness to God.

1 THESSALONIANS 5:16-18 We are called to give thanks in all circumstances.

(See also: Blessings)

Trials

Matthew 11:28-30 Christ promises us rest for our souls.

John 15:18 Jesus understands our struggles.

John 16:33 We can have peace in trials.

Romans 5:1-5 Trials help us learn to endure.

Romans 8:28 God causes everything to work together for the good of his people.

2 Corinthians 6:3-13 Believers can expect to suffer for their faith.

James 1:2-4 God can use trials to help us grow.

(See also: Suffering)

Trust

Philippians 1:6 We can trust God to complete the good work he has begun in us.

(See also: Doubts, Faith)

Truth

John 8:31-32 The truth will set us free.

John 14:6 Jesus Christ is the truth.

John 17:17 God's Word is truth.

1 John 1:5-7 We must not only believe the truth but also live by it.

Unbelievers

John 17:14-19 Christians are called to live holy lives among unbelievers.

ROMANS 8:9 Unbelievers do not have the Holy Spirit.

2 CORINTHIANS 6:14-18 We should avoid situations that force us to compromise our beliefs.

1 JOHN 5:10-12 Believing in Jesus Christ is essential for eternal life.

Unity
JOHN 17:21 Living in unity for Christ will help the world to believe in him.

ROMANS 12:9-16 Unity includes bearing one another's joys and burdens.

1 CORINTHIANS 1:10 Believers must seek unity in Christ.

EPHESIANS 4:3-13 There can be great unity even in great diversity.

PHILIPPIANS 1:3-11 The love Christ commanded should create unity among believers.

PHILIPPIANS 2:1-2 Unity ought to be a distinctive mark among Christians.

Using your abilities wisely
MATTHEW 25:15-23, 29 We are called to use our resources to benefit God's Kingdom.

LUKE 12:48 God expects more from those who have been given more.

JOHN 3:27-28 We must maintain proper humility regarding our abilities.

ROMANS 12:6-8 Discover your abilities and then use them to serve Christ.

EPHESIANS 4:7-12 God has given all believers a special gift to build up the church.

1 PETER 4:10-11 Use your abilities to help others and glorify God.

(See also: Gifts)

Wisdom

MATTHEW 7:24-27 Wise people build on the solid foundation of Christ's teaching.

ACTS 7:9-15 Joseph was given great wisdom from God.

1 CORINTHIANS 2:1-16 God's wisdom is different from the world's wisdom.

JAMES 1:5 God will give us wisdom if we ask for it.

Witnessing

MATTHEW 5:14-16 Let your good deeds shine so that God may be glorified.

MATTHEW 9:9-13 Jesus came to save sinful people.

MATTHEW 28:16-20 Jesus commands us to make disciples everywhere.

LUKE 12:8-9 If we acknowledge Christ before people, he will acknowledge us.

JOHN 15:27 We are called to tell others about what we have seen in Christ.

ACTS 1:8 Christians are called to spread the gospel across the world.

1 CORINTHIANS 3:5-9 We may plant or water the seed of faith, but only God makes it grow.

1 CORINTHIANS 9:22 Meeting others where they are can help win them to Christ.

2 CORINTHIANS 5:18-21 God has entrusted us with a message we need to share with others.

1 PETER 3:15 Always be ready to explain the reason for your hope.

(See also: Communication, Evangelism, Teaching)

Work

MARK 1:35 Jesus took time out of his busy schedule to pray to the Father.

1 CORINTHIANS 15:58 Our work for God is never wasted.

EPHESIANS 6:5-9 All work should be done as though we are working for God.

Worry

MATTHEW 8:23-27 We do not need to worry when troubles arise.

MATTHEW 10:19-20 We do not need to worry about how to defend ourselves for our faith.

MATTHEW 10:29-31 We do not need to worry since God cares for us.

MATTHEW 14:25-33 We should trust Jesus instead of worrying about our circumstances.

LUKE 12:22-34 Don't worry about clothing or food.

PHILIPPIANS 4:6-18 Instead of worrying, we can give everything to God in prayer.

(See also: Fear, Stress)

Worship

HEBREWS 10:1-10 We can worship because of Christ's sacrifice on our behalf.

HEBREWS 12:28 We should worship with reverence for God.

JAMES 4:8 When we draw near to God, he draws near to us.

Youth

(See: Adolescence)